THE GREAT CLIENT PARTNER

THE

GREAT

CLIENT PARTNER

HOW SOFT SKILLS ARE
THE TRUE CURRENCY
IN CLIENT RELATIONSHIPS

JARED BELSKY

MAHOPAC
PUBLISHING

www.thegreatclientpartner.com

THE GREAT CLIENT PARTNER
How Soft Skills Are the True Currency in Client Relationships

ISBN   978-1-5445-0185-7 *Paperback*
        978-1-5445-0093-5 *Ebook*

This book is dedicated to Jeanine, Avner, and Alex. While I do love my job, they are the reason I will always speed home.

CONTENTS

PART THREE: BEHAVE LIKE A LEADER

FOREWORD

**BY BRYAN WIENER, CEO OF COMSCORE
AND FORMER CHAIRMAN AND CEO OF 360i**

The trajectory of my company and career hit an inflection point on an unseasonably cool day in September 2008—the same September that Lehman Brothers collapsed, and the world edged closer toward a Depression greater than anyone had seen since the 1930s. I sat at my desk that afternoon with my thoughts swarming around my fledgling entrepreneurial company, our few hundred employees, and our consumer-spending-dependent clients in retail, travel, and financial services. Was everything we put our money, sweat, and tears into about to go down the toilet as the credit markets froze up, with our clients literally paralyzed by fear?

So I was more than a bit skeptical when Anthony Martinelli, a bigger-than-life character in charge of business development and one of our founders, burst into my office and confidently declared that Jared Belsky was the solution to the hole in the leadership team running our mission critical Atlanta office. I'd met Jared a couple of times socially—his wife had been a previous 360i employee, so he'd attended a few agency events in the past. I knew he had started his career in the agency business, got his MBA, worked at Coca-Cola as a brand manager, and was now in some sort of sales and marketing executive position at a fertilizer company.

I looked up from the spreadsheet showing depressing cash flow scenarios and barked, "You want me to hire a shit salesman to run Atlanta? Are you kidding me?"

Jared was in New York City visiting family that week, so I begrudgingly offered the only time I had available—my hour-long commute home on the Long Island Railroad, which was near where Jared grew up. As we sat on a crowded train, I said, "Jared, I only have one question for you. The economy is collapsing, our clients think the sky is falling, and the country is clearly in for a rough economic ride. Why in the world should I hire you right now?" He paused for what seemed like an eternity. What followed was a persuasive argument that he was the right guy at a pivotal time in the company's history. Jared was not yet qualified perfectly on paper for the job, but it was clear that he had big ambitions, big ideas, and big curiosity. Jared argued passionately that we needed to expand into new verticals like Consumer Packaged Goods, that we needed to graduate from just search to being full-service media, that we needed to up-level and professionalize our workforce, and that it was time to go after even bigger clients with tougher challenges. The part of his response that got him the job was he convinced me he was going to be both a learning and teaching machine, and because of that he was uniquely qualified to play a leading role in scaling this company in what was sure to be a chaotic time.

I'm sure Jared would wholeheartedly agree that over the last ten years, I may have been harder on him than I have been on anyone who ever worked for me. I knew that nurturing his unique combination of talent, introspection, humility, and inspiration would deliver outsized returns for the company and his career. Fortunately for me and everyone else at 360i, this was a great bet.

Marketing used to be a lot easier. You paid close attention to the 4 Ps—product, price, place, and promotion—and if you executed well, you could increase sales even for mediocre products. Those days have changed dramatically along with the shifts in consumer behavior that everyone in marketing is acutely aware of. As a direct result, the role of marketing service firms has changed and been disrupted like never before. Firms need to deliver highly differentiated specialized services to help their clients navigate a highly disruptive business climate while simultaneously figuring out how to grow both their clients' and their own bottom line. Whose job is it to figure out how to keep all these disparate things in alignment? The client partner. A job that has always been tough now requires an array of leadership skills that can seem pretty daunting.

Leadership is a tricky thing. Many people confuse managing a lot of people or having a fancy title with being a leader. This couldn't be further from the truth. In today's marketplace where collaboration is essential, influence—not authority—is the currency of leadership. The simple definition of a leader is one who has willing followers, whether they're your direct reports, coworkers, clients, or partners.

This book is a practical guide to becoming a better leader and navigating a minefield of challenges, from managing cross-functional teams to having difficult conversations with clients, all delivered in easy-to-digest, relatable stories. I recommend you read the book with a notepad (physical or virtual) next to you to consider how you can apply the lessons in real time to your own universe. And then keep the book near your desk and pull it out when you're facing a challenging situation with a client or an employee. It's a good living reminder of the struggles we all deal with as managers and in managing client relationships. Don't worry about getting all thirty-one lessons perfect all the time. God knows, I haven't, and Jared shares many of the lessons born out of mistakes learned at 360i. Just remember, being a great leader is a never-ending, lifelong pursuit.

I have learned so much from Jared over the years, and I'm grateful he has taken the time to provide a framework for sharing lessons learned from a career on the marketing frontlines in the most disruptive period in history. The student has become the teacher with insights that can help us all in our professional and personal lives.

INTRODUCTION

As the CEO of a large marketing communications agency,
I've had the privilege of hosting a group of eight or so new
employees for some candid conversations each month.
They are full of curiosity, wonder, and optimism. I encourage them to ask me any question that might help them
navigate the business or their careers. Over the years, I
have hosted a hundred of these meetings, and they all
have their own unique feel. The question that I seem to
get most often is a flattering but backhanded one, which
amounts to something like, "Hey Jared, how did you get
this gig...when you're still so young?"

First of all, I am reminded by those who love me that I am
no longer all that young. The second and more serious
answer is I have been very fortunate to have had many
people take an active interest in my career, all whom have

helped me understand that very few (if any) skills in the business world are natural.

More fundamentally, they have helped me understand that most things are not intuitive. There is no such thing as a natural leader, just like there is no such thing as a natural Olympic gold medalist or a natural rocket scientist. Soft skills are not soft at all. They are just more nuanced, harder to teach, and harder to learn. In fact, a very rational argument could be made that it's easier to master statistics or coding and perhaps far harder to master how to read a room during a big presentation or give a life-changing review to an employee.

I have spent most of my career in and around communications agencies, Fortune 500 companies, marketing entities, and consultancies, and I can tell you that the secret path to the C-Suite relies on the accumulation of soft skills. The best leaders tend to be vulnerable, are great listeners, are good communicators, have healthy paranoia senses, arbitrate tension well, create trust quickly, motivate others, and speak plainly.

Sadly, in too many circles, that list can be tossed aside as soft skills that come naturally to some and not to others. How many of us have heard someone say, "Well, Billy is a people person. He is just a naturally good listener." We were told that certain folks naturally "put others at ease" or "can sell ice in a snowstorm." Because these things appear to come so easily to some, we got brainwashed into thinking the talents were innate. We also assumed, often with jealousy, that our friends with engineering degrees were smarter and more important.

I am in violent disagreement with that hypothesis. Learning how to be a great listener, for example, is no different than learning how to be a master at using Excel. Each skill can be broken down into parts to practice, use, and optimize until mastery is reached. However, where there are literally thousands of books, courses, and videos on how to master Excel, there are only a handful of credible books on how to be an active listener or to build trust. Further, most of those books tend to be written from a vantage point where everything is seventy-two degrees and sunny, whereas the truth is that soft skills tend to be most useful when things are chaotic, tense, and high stakes. So why is it the case that so few books exist in this area of industry to help people navigate and improve their soft skills?

The problem has three origin points. First, most employees do not realize how critical these softer skills can be. Second, the journey to mastery necessitates self-reflection and vulnerability, and neither are comfortable emotional states for the average worker. Third, there are just not many good books on this topic and even fewer teachers.

We are failing our future leaders. We are taking individual contributors who did well at their craft and putting them in charge of many other young workers. We are then disappointed when they don't lead well. We are surprised during their first review cycle that they demotivate more people than they motivate. We are surprised when they can't seem to arbitrate arguments on their team or they do not know how to run a meeting with twenty people in the room.

If you are reading this book, it is because you want to grow as a leader and ensure you personally invest in more soft-skill acquisition or because you want to find more ways to pass it on to others. Even more specifically, in certain fields like advertising, marketing, creative, consulting, and most marketing communications businesses, the difference between thriving and failure is emotional intelligence and true understanding of those around you.

At the end of the day, what makes a great leader in this business is the ability to deal with the hard things, to anticipate complex moments, and to work around them successfully. Navigating those moments is what defines your career.

Here are some examples of those hard things:

- How to have a conversation with a client about fees they think are too high.

- How to tell an all-star employee they no longer seem to be an all-star.
- How to tell a client you overspent their budget by $220K. Oops.
- How to recognize when your product is poor and when the market beat you.
- How to listen for signals that your business is in trouble.
- How to convey bad news to your boss faster than good news.
- How to indirectly influence creative, production, sales, product, or executive management.
- How to arbitrate an argument between analytics, creative, and media.

It's dealing with those hard things and all the accompanying nuances that inspired me to write this book and share the benefit of all the amazing advice I have received, as well as the lessons I'm still learning.

Whether you work at a services company, an agency, a consultancy, a customer group at a Fortune 500 company, or any company or division that has clients (internal or external) in need of leading, I expect this book will be applicable to you. I hope it's a book you can share with those curious souls you work with who are trying to hone their craft. I have been so lucky to have been taught what seems unteachable, and my main purpose in writing this book is to pay it forward.

PART 1

HONING YOUR SPIDEY SENSE AND IMPROVING YOUR SELF-AWARENESS

LESSON 1

YOUR CLIENT THINKS ABOUT YOU ONLY 5 PERCENT OF THE TIME

"What you need to understand is that my pie chart is the opposite of yours."

—FORMER CLIENT, JEAN PUNDIAK, ASTRAZENECA

When I was twenty-four or so, working at Avenue A (now SapientRazorfish), a leading digital marketing agency, as a hybrid account/media director on the AstraZeneca business, my amazing client, Jean Pundiak, was well overdue (in my mind) to send me approvals on creative display banners to traffic and run. So one Monday morning, I aggressively pursued that permission. Then again on Monday afternoon and on Tuesday afternoon. I was getting worried. Did she not care about her banner ads getting rotated in? I reached out again on Wednesday.

Finally, by Thursday morning, she called and said she'd come over to my offices to chat.

This wouldn't be a big deal, except that I was in New York City and she was hours away in Delaware. I knew whatever she had to say must be important.

She burst into my office the next day and with a slight smile, she proceeded to draw two pie charts on the whiteboard. She carried the wisdom of someone trying to school a well-intentioned twenty-four-year-old.

This is what she drew.

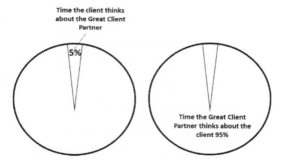

The circle on the left indicates that Jean spent 5 percent of her time focused on me, our agency, and our activities, and she spent 95 percent of her time on other matters, most likely consisting of HR, legal, distribution, PR, sales— and everything else required of her position.

The drawing on the right, meanwhile, was me. It indicated I spent 95 percent of my time thinking about her. She was the queen in my life—my client. The fact that there is such a gap in these pie charts was the crux of her visit.

I had to better understand how to fit my needs as her partner into that smaller available sliver she had available for me. I had to be humble, efficient, and helpful. Not to worry, though. This is only a negative if you are a needy, not self-aware, unconfident client partner. (But that's not you if you are reading this book!)

The worst sin a Great Client Partner can commit is not knowing where they stand or the context for which the battlefield lines are drawn, which can contribute to low self-orientation. Poor self-orientation in the services business is when you are spending too much time focused on your needs and that of your agency versus understanding the client and their ecosystem. It's vitally important to truly grasp the ecosystem in which your client spends their day to better understand where you, your needs, your advice, your requests, and your team fit in.

A Great Client Partner comes to work every morning with one singular goal: to advance the best interests of your client's business in a way that is mutually compatible with your own agency or enterprise. Now, while we strive for mutual benefit (a win-win for the agency and the client), the fact is that the agency must live and die with their client in mind.

This means from the time you wake up until the time your head hits the pillow, you are dreaming and thinking of your clients and their business, and you're parsing every email and every word spoken on the Tuesday status call. "Oh my god, the client just went silent for three seconds and put us on mute. What could that mean?"

We obsess, we parse, we scrutinize, and we even look at short or curt emails and wonder if the client still likes us.

Okay, so what is the issue? What is there to learn here?

The thing to understand is your client is not thinking about you in that same way. This is nothing personal—it's practical. In most cases, your client has a long list of work to do. Theirs is a world that is often bigger than the slice you ever get to see. They have to think about pricing, distribution, HR, career mapping, commodities prices, and the like. In many cases, if your client is a Fortune 1000 company, they experience reorganizations, layoffs, new C-suite leadership shifts—and those things rock their world such that they can't always focus on, say, pushing your new tagline through legal that Thursday. However, you continue to forge ahead, wondering why they simply won't confirm the details you asked for around the fifty-two-person integrated planning meeting coming up on the calendar. You just don't understand how it takes that long for these approvals.

Does this client even care about their own business as much as you do? The answer, surprisingly, is both no and yes. Yes, clients care a great deal about their marketing investment and agency partnership. They want to succeed and want you to succeed. However, clients are not as focused on you as much as you are on them, simply as a function of time constraints and prioritization.

We have to realize that being a true partner means reducing self-orientation and increasing self-awareness. Self-orientation is simply the notion of being inwardly focused at the expense of your clients and team members. You're self-oriented when you are thinking only about your profit and your deadlines and not thinking about all other parties.

The takeaway is not to be any less passionate about your work but rather to think about how you demonstrate empathy and in turn become smarter about how and when you communicate.

- Think about emailing early or late in the day when your clients are less frenzied and better able to find time to respond.

- Think about subject lines that make your requests clear and easy to respond to.
- Think about getting buy-in (versus tell-in) for all timelines.
- Think about your tone and if you demonstrate empathy.
- Think about managing your own team's paranoia such that urgency never crosses into anger or passive aggressiveness.

Mastering the significance of the two pie charts in this chapter is a practical and visual way to better grasp this truth of understanding where you stand and how best to maximize the client-agency relationship from an expectation management perspective.

THREE HABIT CHANGES

1. Understand how your client maps their day. Work to ask for approvals during their calmer hours (perhaps early morning) and work to engage in more important dialogue during business hours, which are traditionally done via appointment and better done early in the morning or at the end of the day.
2. Use subject lines effectively. "Action Required Please: Quick Approval Request" vs. "Let's Talk about Creative Approvals."
3. If you want to guarantee your client sees something,

then send it FedEx overnight to their desk. People always open their own FedEx deliveries.

YOUR FROM → TO PERSONAL GOAL:

FROM a leader who obsesses about why a client is not returning calls or emails, TO a leader who empathizes with your client's other priorities to get the most out of the relationship.

LESSON 2

GET OUT OF YOUR IVORY TOWER AND INTO THE STORES

"Get up there into the rafters and pack down some fertilizer pellets."

—JON ROSENTHAL, FORMER PRESIDENT
AND OWNER, DYNAMITE PLANT FOOD

If you want the client to consider you part of their inner circle, don't view their business through a detached, academic lens. Get to know what they do intimately.

The Great Client Partner needs to understand the product and the business they are dealing with in a very detailed way. They need to understand how the product is used and consumed—even where it sits on a shelf. Too often, marketers know about their client's products only via paper briefs and larger PowerPoint "decks" (also known as slide presentations).

Further, to be a good marketer, the Great Client Partner must have a deep understanding of the logistics of the business they are trying to lead.

POLE SIGNS

When I was in brand management at the Coca-Cola Company, working on the Fanta business, I wanted to make an impact. I was assigned to work on our Out-Of-Home signage (or OOH, which refers to advertising that consumers see out in the world, as opposed to on their televisions or in their magazines) to ensure our pole signs were more cutting edge. I took this assignment on with the trademark relish of a stubborn Ivy League kid out to prove that his pole sign creation would most assuredly be the thing to reshape the entire Coca-Cola Company.

I started by creating a brief to develop the most amazing, most cutting-edge pole sign ever designed. Surely, I would be the guy to create the one pole sign that got people driving at fifty-five miles per hour past a gas station to pull in and buy a Fanta twenty-ounce because of my superior orange color choice. With optimism, I pushed forward, and we found a vendor that would make a bright orange, glow-in-the-dark, glitter-based OOH masterpiece that could go on the poles at the gas stations, ensuring Fanta would stick out.

Flash forward about six months. While still working at the Coca-Cola Company, I was lucky enough to take two weeks in the field working in West Philadelphia, where a ton of Fanta was sold. I was riding along in this huge Coke/Fanta truck with the driver, a good-natured, straight-shooting guy I'll call Gus. We drove his route, and I did my part to lift six-packs of Fanta in the blazing Philly summer heat. I was really just trying not to embarrass myself as my small arms got lost in the shadows created by Gus's huge biceps.

Since I was doing my best, I got the sense that I was earning a bit of Gus's respect, even if it was through sympathy. In the second week of my ride-along, we passed a gas station that—sure enough—featured a pole sign of my genius creation.

Gus said, "You see that, Jared? That's what I was talking about. Advertising folks never think about the damn logistics or the real-freaking-world. They're always up in their ivory tower."

Gulping, I asked what he meant. Sure enough, he pointed at this pole sign that was now completely weather-beaten: muted orange, dull, the words barely visible.

"Jared," Gus said, "do you know what's outside?"

I said, "Uh, I don't know what you mean."

"What's outside is *weather*, Jared, all sorts. Sun, rain, and wind," Gus laughed in my direction. He went on to explain that pole signs need to take into account that weather, and that any brand guy who had logged the right time in the field would have understood this. The point is I simply did not spend enough time getting dirt under my fingernails to understand how the business runs. I should have gone out to look at gas station pole signs, understand weather effects, and really appreciate the physical world.

After Coca-Cola, I worked with a friend in the fertilizer business to try to upend Miracle-Gro. We saw a huge opportunity to design a more beautiful bottle than the old functional bottles we started with. We thought there could be beauty in these new bottles. As head of marketing, I was lucky to have a very supportive owner (and now friend) named Jon Rosenthal, who encouraged me to make unique packaging that really popped. With the help of a great team, we did indeed achieve that, as you can see in these before-and-after shots.

Incorporating a unique bottle shape, full coverage with the label, and bright, illustrative plant photos went a long way to making the packaging more beautiful.

But beautiful should have been just one part of the equation. Turns out that fertilizer goes through hell at a Home Depot. It sits in one-hundred-degree weather in Arizona and thirty-degree weather in Alaska. It gets nicked by pallet lifts and mashed under the weight of huge bags of grass seed. Long story short, the ink we ended up sourcing did not hold up under the stress of that weather, and the plastic could not take that sort of impact. Six months into the sales season, we had a lot of damaged product we had to take back or replace. Jon reminded me about the value of getting up in the rafters and packing down fertilizer, which meant I had to get dirty to understand the industry and the conditions.

I probably spent one hundred hours that next year volunteering at greenhouses and garden centers with Jon as my inspiration. I got to really understand the business, and this changed my viewpoint forever.

The importance of immersing yourself in your client's business is a lesson that can be learned. But if you went on a factory tour a few times and maybe had to put on safety goggles—don't kid yourself. That's not immersion. You know it when you do it right.

THREE HABIT CHANGES

1. Get out into the field. Live near your product's point of sale. Do you know how it does in the elements? How does it ship? What does it do on the shelf?

2. Before ever releasing a product, make sure you speak to people in the field. Go to your Publix, your GameStop, your Home Depot, or your convenience mart and speak to the folks in the stores, at the cash registers, or to the folks packing out the box store at two in the morning. You will learn a lot from these amazing people.

3. Volunteer for a while—whatever time you can spare— to really experience what things look like for your client's products at the retail level. A client leader I knew actually got a job bagging groceries at a supermarket for a month to gain information on how things looked at the store level.

YOUR FROM → TO PERSONAL GOAL:

FROM being a leader who gives commands from a point

of academia and Excel sheets, TO being a leader who spends more time in the stores, with your customers, in the field, and in the factories of your clients.

BONUS HABIT CHANGE

Bonus: Field Awareness Exercise

Check your team's awareness. Administer this quiz to your extended internal team. For anyone who gets less than 90 percent correct, you should assume they don't know nearly enough about your client's business for you to truly earn the right to call yourself a business partner. If you are the leader of your team, copy the chart below, print it out, and start off your next meeting by administering this fun little test. The scores are not the point; what matters is that you can now engage your team in a dialogue about how well (or poorly) you collectively know of that key client about whom you thought you knew everything.

QUESTION	ANSWER	
How does your client make their product or execute their service?		
How does your client make money? What is the value stream on both sides of the ledger (costs and revenue)?		
What does it take for the product/service to arrive at store/web?		
At street-level (if applicable), what are the top three challenges they face?		
How is their competition hurting their business at the street level? What is happening at the shelf-battle level?		
Have you attended at least three of the four quarterly conference calls this year?		
What is the biggest threat to your client's margin?		
Do you understand (truly) how the entire sales process works from start to finish?		

LESSON 3

THE STATEMENT OF WORK IS NOT THE BIBLE

You are a privileged custodian of your client's time, work, and assets.

At the heart of the time-management debate lies a critical misunderstanding, which becomes the cancer that erodes so many great client-agent relationships. This concept is about who owns the hours. It's easy to think that since the agency manages the projects, the agency also owns the hours—but actually the agency is merely the steward of those hours. The time was purchased by the client, who now fully owns them.

Really the core issue here is trust. How will you handle the client's hours? If you have ever been around a creative agency or consultancy, you will frequently hear phrases like, "They are burning up our hours," or, "Don't they care about how I use my time?"

It's a fair question and one that the Great Client Partner should have a good answer to. That requires leadership, and as it relates to time, there are three areas to lead in:

- Help your team understand that the hours belong to the client and they are the custodian.
- If you treat their hours like your own personal money and ensure continual alignment of interests, you will do great things.
- Treat each hour like an investment unit. Be purposeful. If purpose is your North Star, then having healthy conflict with your clients will be welcomed.

MANAGING TIME AS IT RELATES TO THE SOW

The best advice I can dispense here is to understand the Statement of Work (SOW) that you have in place with your client is the source of most poor behaviors. Too many people look at a SOW like it's the Bible when it should be treated like the Constitution. The Bible (regardless of your thoughts about it) was written thousands of years ago and cannot be changed. The Constitution, by contrast, is a document that was meant to be amended, changed, debated, and argued about by humans.

Often, you write your SOW when you know nothing about your client. Too often, what I see are relationships governed by SOWs drafted during your courtship years when you knew nothing about each other's goals. Or, more specifically, drafted right after a pitch when your knowledge of a client's business needs hovered at around two on a scale of one to ten. But a SOW can even be misleading in a mature relationship.

I once saw a SOW that existed to govern a social media relationship. This was in 2012 (the very early days of social media, so excuse the quaintness of this story) when the vanguard was to gain maximum followers and fans. I have altered the numbers below for simplicity's sake, but they still exist to prove a point. Let's just pretend this was a $600K annual SOW to help manage social channels. It was for the management of Facebook, YouTube, and Twitter, on the assumption they were of roughly equal importance at that moment in time to this particular client. Some fourteen months later, we woke up when we got a call from the client, who asked us, with some hint of aggravation, "How many Twitter followers do we have?"

My face got red as I realized the answer was a measly 138 Twitter followers. In other words, for a good deal of money, we were creating content and doing hard work that spoke to only 138 followers. The original intention was not the issue. The issue and the shame were in not realizing this much earlier and suggesting a change in the SOW that would represent a better match between costs and value to the client. You see, the failure was not having only 138 followers (that was a channel issue), but rather, we did not bring this to their attention as the wrong prioritization of their investment dollars. In this example, the team lacked self-awareness. The team had their heads down working so hard on the task at hand that nobody stopped to ask the larger questions. Self-awareness requires the deft ability to pause and ask questions as to how your actions fit into the bigger picture and how they are being perceived. I asked the account director at the time, and she truthfully commented she was ensuring we lived up to the SOW and our commitments. Her honesty, her hard work, and her commitment to the client was not in question. The lesson was that she let the SOW be the tail that wagged the dog.

A Great Client Partner owns the SOW and can use it, bend it, and shape it over time. A Great Client Partner stewards the SOW, questions it, and ensures it always provides mutual wins for both the agent and client. A Great Client Partner in this situation recognizes the SOW is not in rhythm with the needs of the moment and offers to change and evolve it as needed. In this example, we should have focused more of our resources, dollars, and time on the channels that were working and should have suggested we pause work on the Twitter account.

Ultimately, all the right behaviors start with realizing you are the custodian of your client's hours. As a leader, you might be challenged to find some sort of way to turn this knowledge into a rally cry. At 360i, we did this by summoning wisdom from the late John Wooden, the famous basketball coach who framed it as "don't mistake activity for achievement." Too often in the services business, we are proud to show off our checklist of all the things we have done. Too often, it is just a list of things. Demand that you and the people you work with understand whether or not those are indeed needle-moving things.

THREE HABIT CHANGES

1. Vocabulary change: never call them "your hours." They belong to the client.
2. Look at your SOW every six months or so and find ways to proactively amend or adapt it. Make this a ritual you do with your clients. If nothing else, have a healthy discussion with the client about what's working and what could be adjusted. Don't let the SOW ever become toxic to your project.
3. Do a benefit analysis. What percentage of the retained hours in the past three months were geared toward achievement versus task completion?

YOUR FROM → TO PERSONAL GOALS:

FROM a leader who lets the paperwork (contracts, SOWs) in their relationships guide the output, TO a leader who focuses on what moves the needle and makes that their true north.

FROM a leader who values activity, TO a leader who values aligned achievement.

LESSON 4

HEALTHY PARANOIA WILL DRIVE YOU TO SUCCEED

One of my favorite stories that I have applied to my career and retaught countless times comes from a very quantitatively oriented economics book called *The Black Swan* by Nassim Nicholas Taleb. The story is about a turkey.

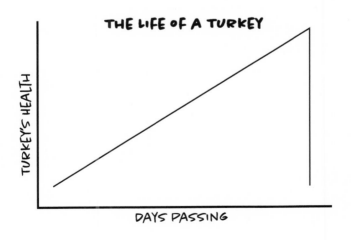

THE LIFE OF A TURKEY

TURKEY'S HEALTH

DAYS PASSING

This chart is essentially the life story of Tom the Turkey. In the simplest terms, it's about a turkey who is very skeptical of the humans around him as he first enters the turkey farm, but over time, he grows fatter and happier. He gets lazy, loves being fed, loves his turkey friends, and ignores anything that signals a problem, like the fact that some of his friends are starting to disappear.

As days and years go by, his confidence is growing. He gets more food. He gets fatter. On the day right before his demise, he is technically at his peak confidence.

And then, boom: death.

What happened? Thanksgiving happened! However, all the key performance indicators were telling Tom the Turkey he was thriving. This happens to us all.

I was leading an account named Ancestry.com for a period of time as executive sponsor. I loved this brand (and still do). Our team was absolutely crushing the business goals. We were beating the forecast on volume (subscriptions) and also beating the forecast on efficiency (cost per subscription). Each quarterly business review that went by, we would travel to San Francisco, have a great meeting and lean back, pleased at our chart, which went up and to the right.

You know that chart? The one where volume is going up

and up and up. We were certain we were killing it. Then, one day, out of the blue (or was it?), the client called me to tell me they were taking the work in-house to handle it themselves.

How did we not see this coming?

Well, two things were going on: (1) false positives and (2) not looking for clues. To the first guilty charge, we kept cheering our achievements on volume of subscriptions. However, results alone do not make a healthy partnership. We were not leading them enough, perhaps, in strategy, or thought leadership.

To the second guilty charge, I was simply not looking for clues. Each quarter that went by, the client was adding head count to their roster. An analytics person here, a search person here, a project manager there. We could have seen it, but we had blinders on. We were not looking for warning signals because there was so much good, and that was all we wanted to see.

To some degree, I was Tom. And as a good friend of mine, Anthony Martinelli often says in quoting *The Godfather*, "Tom...you're out." Indeed, Tom was out. Tom was getting steak knives.

What can the Great Client Partner in training learn from

this? The lesson is simple: beware of looking at false positives. Look for what could be wrong or what could be better.

I would also offer up that you try and use the "Contract for Client-Centric Healthy Paranoia" at the end of this chapter. This is something you can ask those who you manage to fill out. It forces them to go through the exercise of thinking deeply about what could be wrong versus what appears to be wrong on the surface. It then focuses the person on creating new wins or thought leadership not in response to an issue, but in the spirit of getting ahead.

THREE HABIT CHANGES

1. Provide clients the chance to give anonymous feedback every six months via a report card.
2. Have internal healthy-paranoia sessions each quarter with your team where you purposefully look for what could be wrong versus just celebrating what's going right.
3. Make sure the relationship is about more than just results (fleeting) and more about thought leadership. Thought leadership is enduring. It means your client thinks about you or your company when they need to solve a tough business challenge. It's an elastic compliment. As the client changes, they still come to you to solve those thorny challenges.

YOUR FROM → TO PERSONAL GOAL:

FROM a leader who thinks things are going too well for there to be a problem, TO a leader who looks for subtle signals about relationship health when and where others don't think to pay attention.

A CONTRACT FOR CLIENT-CENTRIC HEALTHY PARANOIA

Three things I or my team will commit to over the next sixty days to more aggressively and uniquely sniff out potential issues that might exist with my client:

1.

2.

3.

Three things I or my team will do to generate more thought leadership credibility and stay ahead of client issues, even though there is nothing wrong right now:

1.

2.

3.

LESSON 5

PREPARE TO PRESENT

Public speaking is hard. If you're not proficient at it yet, don't let anyone try to make you feel better by patting you on the back and telling you, "It will come with time." It won't. It's just hard. It requires practice and perseverance.

When I was twenty-seven and in the first year of my MBA program at Emory in Atlanta, I was part of a four-person team that won an *Amazing Race*-like charity drive where teams raised money for a nonprofit without having a single dollar in startup funds.

After a short moment of euphoria at our success, I learned I would have to present the story of our victory to over one thousand people at Emory during the ceremony. I got up to the podium, started to speak, and only a whisper came out. Shortly after, sweat came out...and continued to come out. My blue shirt betrayed me, and my armpits were clearly flooding with anxiety. To this day, I try and avoid blue dress shirts.

So now I was a whispering, sweating, nervous fool. It got worse—there appeared to be a vice on that podium, squeezing the life out of me. I can't prove its existence, but I can tell you for damned sure it was pressing on my chest cavity and not allowing me to speak. I made my remarks short and rushed off the stage. I resolved to become an eight-out-of-ten in public speaking within five years.

The number one issue in terms of self-awareness for Great Client Partners is often the divide between how great they assume they are at being persuasive and how good they actually are.

How you communicate is critical to your job as a Great Client Partner. However, most client leaders simply wing it. Great leaders have the ability to change the trajectory of relationships, campaigns, brands, and teams with a thoughtfully prepared speech and presentation. For every important speech or talk you have to give, you should consider having a routine. A routine is a good way to condition yourself for optimal performance for these situations. Routines and habits help you develop until something becomes natural.

Here are six steps that have worked for me, for your consideration:

- **Step 1:** *Write an abstract*—This should be a paragraph that encapsulates the essence of the presentation you envision giving. This abstract also has a dual purpose of aligning your goals with your constituents. Whether you're presenting to a demanding boss or stressed-out peers, writing an abstract allows you to understand and agree on the essence of the presentation before getting to the outline, or PowerPoint.
- **Step 2:** *Write a bulleted outline*—This piece of the process is literally typing out ten or more things that your presentation must do and in what prioritized order. These bullets should nail the key points you are going to try and make and note any supporting detail that you might have or that you might need to gather.
- **Step 3:** *The script*—Write out a table that looks like the one that follows on page 55. This will be your full talk track, which is essentially what you plan to say during the big day, word-for-word, accompanied by your ideal visual that would populate a slide in your deck (see the table that follows; the "Script" column should be a specific script as though you could deliver the perfect words on the big day). This ritual has two purposes. First, writing this out in a Word document format allows for faster iteration and changes with your collaborators. It is interesting, but once you build a slide,

you are less likely to make meaningful changes due to the cost of labor. Changing words on a page is far easier. Second, writing a script allows you to develop your true speech and talk flow, whereas a PowerPoint focuses you on visuals, and then you neglect the flow, often until it's too late.

After you've done steps 1 to 3, it's time to rehearse. These next three steps are all about moving you away from actually reading anything during your presentation and making you seem natural and freely able to respond to the challenges of the presentation environment.

- **Step 4:** *Practice*—Take your script, read it, and rehearse it a minimum of seven times. Use a mirror for the first five and use a friend or loved one for the last two. If you don't have anyone nearby, then film yourself—it's just a way to add a bit of pressure and realism.
- **Step 5:** *Refine*—Throw out that script and reduce each slide on the talk track to two "trigger bullets," written on index cards. In other words, if the script you were trying to remember reads, "There are huge tailwinds in the internet advertising business as marketers shift budgets from linear television to Facebook, Google, and other data-driven options chosen for their target ability and accountability," then make your bullets on your card simply read "tailwinds" and "shift to data-driven options." This way, you can focus on those two

areas, and the details will fill themselves in. If you continue to memorize your script word for word, then the minute you forget just one word, you will freeze up.

- **Step 6:** *Repeat*—Practice a couple more times just with the index cards. Remember, you threw away your script, and you are in the flow now.

And now you are ready.

SCRIPT TABLE

SLIDE	SCRIPT	VISUAL
1	Welcome to our offices. Thank you for coming to learn more about our team, culture, and our offerings around data-reporting, dashboarding, and data visualization.	Picture of a CMO dashboard
2	Today, we will be discussing three key areas. First, we will focus on getting clean data. Second, we will discuss the data-visualization options available. Third, we will discuss how to weigh options across efficacy and cost.	Bulleted text highlighting the three key aspects of today's conversation
3	Getting clean data requires proper usage of APIs as well as having someone on your staff with the ability to manipulate the data into a way that is organized correctly into tables.	Visualization of clean and structured data organized into tables.

One parting note just to reemphasize. There is a huge secondary advantage to writing out your talk in this manner of a grid, which is buy-in. Giving a big talk or speech is, by itself, already really hard. Risking nonalignment with your boss would simply be even more nerve-wracking. By creating a slide-by-slide script, you can share this draft early in the process. This is far more preferable to you thinking you have created some oratorical masterpiece which your boss has not yet blessed. This scripting grid will save you. Embrace it.

THREE HABIT CHANGES

1. Start off your next big talk preparation with a series of simple bullets on what the essence of your talk is about.
2. Utilize a script grid.
3. Get buy-in early from your boss or partners using your script grid so you can feel confident everyone is in the tent with you and cheering for you.

YOUR FROM → TO PERSONAL GOAL:

FROM a leader who communicates instinctually, TO a leader who prepares in a purposeful manner for each opportunity.

LESSON 6

ORGANIZE EFFECTIVE ARGUMENTS

As an aspiring Great Client Partner, one of your main jobs is to advocate. To advocate for the work you represent, to advocate for resources for your team, or to advocate for more compensation from your client so you can, in turn, do better work. I have been observing how client leaders make arguments in the interest of advocacy for almost twenty years, and it occurs to me these arguments are often haphazard and very emotional in nature.

Learning how to advocate in a rigor-based manner is not easy, but there is a methodology. Next, you see the CRER formula: Context, Risk/Reward, Economics, and Recommendation.

Like any story, there is a narrative arc to a good flow

1. Content / Exec Summary
2. Risk vs. Reward
3. Economics (80/20
4. Recommendation / Timing

Let's take this methodology for a spin and use a very common situation for a client leader at a consulting company, agency, or any services or sales organization, who is advocating for internal resources to get a "sizzle reel" or video case study created. A sizzle reel is essentially a video of greatest hits which allows you to help the client see how much great work you have produced in a very exciting and positive light. They cost upwards of $10,000 sometimes (when you include soft costs), so the investment is one that typically needs approval by someone on the executive team. I chose this particular marketing request to role-play, because it is a very common request in our world, and many team leaders want to create these.

Here are two scenarios:

BEFORE THE "CRER" METHODOLOGY

Dear Jared, I have this killer idea to make a video for this upcoming meeting that will make it way, way better. It's a very important meeting with a very senior guy. I think if we make this video, it will impress him and get us some more attention. We need to turn it around in four days, but it will be worth it. Trust me on this one. Let's make the investment! #awesomevideo #comeonjared #sayyes!

AFTER THE "CRER" METHODOLOGY

- **Context/Executive Summary:** 360i is finally getting in front of the SVP of US Acquisition, who only knows us in a very tactical way and has never seen our work in its most flattering light. As such, we want to share a five-minute sizzle reel with him to make Search, Display, and Analytics appear as big as we know them to be. During the last quarter, our margin profile was healthy, as was team morale.

- **Risk/Reward Profile:** This is a $10 million client, and the meeting is with the head of the entire piece of business, which comprises $8.5 million of the total. There is an RFP coming in October. The risk is that he continues to think of us as small ball. The reward is the ability for him to see us as his lead thought partner who has driven their business in the past and into the future.

- **Economics:** This video will have:

- $8,000 in hard costs (production, etc.)
- $2,000 in soft costs
- Ten hours of blended resources at $200/hour

(Note: This is 80/20 economics because it's not tortured math. This is not getting into a more complicated breakdown of all costs, such as listing the production costs, for example. It's not that understanding isn't important—it is—but at times, that level of detail can delay or cloud the argument.)

- **Recommendation:** I am asking for an executive sign-off in the form of go/no-go by Wednesday.

As you can see, the argument in the second example, after the CRER, is far more buttoned up and easy to follow, and an executive can more easily weigh in with an answer. Practice this and make it a habit, and you will find your ability to get decisions in your favor will increase.

Given that this chapter sits within the larger premise of improving your self-awareness, the true key learning here is that executives are very busy. Your clients or your own CEO has no time for long and complex arguments. They have to size up 500+ emails per day, use clues available to them, and make tough calls. Your ability to succeed will increase if you can get them exactly what they need, and no more, in the fewest number of words. The CRER format will remind you to focus on the key elements.

THREE HABIT CHANGES

1. Practice the CRER methodology every time you ask for resources.
2. Become proficient with 80/20 economics by understanding how money in your business is made, both in general and as it relates to you specifically, and where the costs are.
3. Work with your team to structure emails with CRER to clients when you are asking them for anything—from copy approval to green-lighting of a campaign—and you will find response time gets cut in half.

YOUR FROM → TO PERSONAL GOAL:

FROM being a leader who makes an argument rooted in emotion, TO a leader that uses a simple and principled method for making an argument.

LESSON 7

BE COMFORTABLE TALKING ABOUT FINANCES

Words matter.

As a Great Client Partner, being thoughtful about your word choices is critical. It sets the tone for your team, but also decides how your team presents itself to the client. When it comes to money and financials, word choice is exponentially important. Humans are very awkward when it comes to money conversations. This discomfort is rooted in lack of education and practice. Thankfully, both of those issues can be resolved. First, let's talk about creating a better service-industry financial vocabulary, and then let's spend time talking through some common financial discussions you can prepare for in advance.

Here are some commonly used phrases that tend to be deadly if used incorrectly, and a few great substitute choices.

OFFENSIVE FINANCE TERM	DANGER OF WORD	NEW TERM	WHY?
Burning Hours	Creates a feeling that hours are tossed in the garbage or lit on fire.	Utilization, Pacing	Refocuses the conversation on how the hours are being used, not that they are burning hot.
Small Client	Allows certain folks at the agency to believe the client is not important.	Growth Client	Allows you to reposition the client as one where you can be nimble and pilot new ideas and ways you work. There is no such thing as a small client.

The Great Client Partner, though, does not just have to focus on wording in front of their team; they also need to have some very difficult conversations around money with procurement, partners, and clients. That could fill its own book, so instead, I am going to select the largest and most common trap questions and deconstruct some very modern approaches to answers that create productive debate.

1. **Most Common Procurement/Client Objection:** Your rates seem very expensive!
2. **What is going on?** Procurement or your client is

signaling to you that you are expensive. This is very common and could very well be true. In this economic environment, you will always hear this. It might be real (you are too expensive), it could be psychological (it feels your hand is always out), or it could be even bad information (as in the client just does not have ideal data for their objection). Whatever the case, perception is reality in the services business.

3. **What is the issue?** "Expensive" is a relative term. As the Great Client Partner, you need to find out how the client defines "expensive," get better information, and ultimately try and steer the conversation to value. Value is a great topic around which to align. Value can be debated.

4. **How the Great Client Partner deals with this question:**

   ◦ "We are very comfortable that our billable rates offer great value to our clients, relative to the industry. We've benchmarked these against the 4A's comp survey, and we know our people are much better and more expensive than the average agency. We are always happy to talk about value, team construction, overall FTE allocations by position, and work together to find the right team that can win and move the needle against the assignment that the client gives us. We would love to talk about value together. I would ask, kindly, if we can learn how you view us as expensive, though.

Is that relative to the other agencies who work with you? Is that relative to a benchmarking survey you have? Can you help us better contextualize this? Do we have too much account and too little analytics support? Are we too senior with not enough junior support?"

○ By moving to these questions, you are working together with your client or procurement person to solve the real problem. This is not about tricks. You can't trick your client or procurement. They are smart. They actually want to work with you and solve things with you, but first you both need to invest in understanding where you are coming from.

Beyond speaking to procurement, your other financial role as a client leader is understanding what levers you can pull to improve the health of the client. Many leaders make the mistake of assuming there is little they can do—this could not be more wrong (in a good way). See the chart that follows to understand the full nature of the levers available to you as the client leader to improve the health of the account.

Margin (Business Health) Drivers

Revenue	• Define clear scope, objectives, and goals prior to beginning project
	• Secure client approval before projects begin
	• Secure SOW approval
	   • Will ensure proper pricing
	   • Will enable efficient and timely staffing
	   • Will satisfy "persuasive evidence"

Agency Absorptions	• Establish dedicated teams where possible • Secure retainers when possible • Eliminate surprises: keep the client in the loop with real time updates
Unbillable Labor	• Secure SOW approval • Accurate time reporting is critical • Minimize the amount of "unpaid" work • Have internal conversations on all new projects and investments before engaging
Client Non Pass-Through	• Secure client approval for all pass-through costs, prior to incurring costs • Review billable/non-billable expense reports and ensure billing with budget trackers • Be thoughtful about travel expenses

The notion in this chart is that the Great Client Partner can indeed affect a lot of change, and that change comes in several buckets. For Revenue, this is your ability to either grow the business, or at least grow the health of the business, by smart Statement of Work creation, good team construction, accurate timesheet compliance, and being smart about investment work. For Unbillable Labor, there are going to be times when it makes sense to invest into the business and do a solid for the client but keep track of how often you do so and be thoughtful and rigorous in terms of how you justify when to go beyond the scope.

As the client leader, you also can control costs by being thoughtful and prudent about travel expenses. The point is, there is much you can control. I see so many client leaders upset about what they don't control, but few realize how much of a difference they can make on practical matters.

Dealing with money and finance is a tricky thing for a client leader. On the one hand, you need to be a great steward of your agency business. You need to look out for your team, their hours, and the overall health of the business. On the other hand, you need to service the client and understand there are times when overinvestment is critical or when waiving a data-overage fee is just needed to preserve and extend trust. Financial management in the advertising world is not the same as being a CPA, largely because knowing what counts can be a bit more subjective.

There is a great Einstein quote that goes, "Not everything that counts can be counted, and not everything that can be counted, counts." The point is sort of like saying, "Know what matters in your metrics, and know what matters to the client, and focus there." Don't worry about every single penny on either side to the point that it clouds your judgment. Be smart, but never be penny wise and pound foolish. Money conversations make, or more often break, relationships.

THREE HABIT CHANGES

1. Avoid ever using the word "profitability" around your larger team to focus on the work and team morale. Instead, use words like "client health."
2. Practice procurement conversations before they actually happen by role-playing with a team member.
3. At the end of every month, find time to look back to see if you've used the drivers in the previous chart

to improve the health of the client and teams you manage.

YOUR FROM → TO PERSONAL GOAL:

FROM a leader who is clumsy around financial vocabulary, TO a leader who is confident and purposeful.

LESSON 8

DON'T PROTECT TERRITORY, SEEK PRODUCTIVITY

"I would rather have a smaller piece of something bigger than a larger piece of something smaller."

—MICHAEL COHN, FOUNDER OF CLOUD SHERPAS AND MANAGING DIRECTOR OF TECHSTARS ATLANTA

I have begun this chapter with a quote from a close friend of mine, someone who is in the technology and start-up space. He was a founder of Cloud Sherpas, a company that had a great exit to Accenture, and then he became Managing Director of Techstars Atlanta. As founder of Cloud Sherpas, Michael had a tough choice. He could stay as CEO of his company, focus on territory and title, or he could bring in the people needed to get it to the next level and focus on productivity.

Michael chose the second, and he'll always be an inspiration to me and others for that move. This was a choice of productivity over territory on the grandest of stages with so much at stake.

The good client leader is trained to grow their accounts. A Great Client Partner knows that growing your account means growing the client's business. Further, it means that, on occasion, you might need to shrink your own remit in order to preserve your agency's relevance, trustworthiness, and long-term ability to grow.

There was a very important client we worked with at the agency: AARP. They were a client for whom we did certain areas of performance digital media, including Search Engine Optimization (SEO). It was a very healthy relationship, and one that lasted for almost seven years. The senior clients were incredibly supportive, kind, and smart. They pushed us hard and raised our goals each year for traffic and quality of visitors, and each year our amazing team beat those goals. A very healthy relationship indeed.

I was executive sponsor on the piece of business (the accountable executive), so I remember it very well. As time went on, I began to understand that from the client's perspective, we were viewed as incredible partners and custodians of their media budgets. However, as a content company, they began to realize they needed to invest more money internally on their own content destiny. They hired content and SEO experts to keep this very important area close to their business. As they staffed up, we could tell that something was changing in terms of how they viewed our SEO practice. They felt that our recommendations were strong, but they realized their destiny was to own more of this in-house and to go with a different model. There were hints along the way, but we did not see them.

Finally, one day, the call came. In any services industry, you know this call. It's the call where your client tells you something is not working out. It feels horrible every time. But if you use those calls as a learning opportunity, they can be instructive. This was no exception. My takeaway from my call with my contact there, Nataki, who was head of their digital operations, was simple. They were starting to feel that for this one service, SEO, the match was no longer there, and it was starting to spill over into the broader relationship. I asked her for twenty-four hours to think.

Nataki is a rare client who can deliver bad news in a way that still feels fair and compassionate. Still, it stung. After picking myself up off the ground, I talked it over with my team. What we all realized in that moment was that we had better fire ourselves from SEO in order to save the bigger and more important relationship. Sure, we could have fought! We could have showed where we had been successful for them, putting ourselves on probation. We could have doubled down on the team and resources, and put together an innovation roadmap or something sexy to demonstrate renewed focus.

Instead, we took a step back. We thought about mutual alignment. Alignment is an extremely important issue for a Great Client Partner. (There's a whole lesson devoted to it later in the book.)

AARP, at heart, is a content provider. And content is the heart of SEO. It was easy to realize it was in this client's best interests to bring SEO in-house. We also realized it was in our interest to be loved for what we did well for them. I called Nataki the next day, and we both acknowledged it was time to move on from this service line.

Nataki respected our self-awareness (win!), and our financial health on the account actually went up (win-win!) because we were no longer having to spend so many good hours chasing something where our efforts were not hitting the mark.

A Great Client Partner always thinks about true win-wins for themselves as the service provider/partner and for their client alike. A client services hack, who always provides a yes to the client—or worse, only fights for the agency—is missing half the picture. Everything should be judged by finding a win for both sides. It is always the case that there is mutual alignment to fight for which ensures the longest and most sustainable relationships.

The focus must be on productivity, not territory.

ONE HABIT CHANGE

Take stock in what is going really well in your relationship with your client. Don't look simply to protect the remit. Look at what you can give back to forge long-term trust. At minimum, once per year, you have a natural time to review your contract and scope. Take the time, in partnership with your client, to evaluate each service you are providing and ask some basic questions:

- Should I start doing something new? Should the agency be doing less of one service and lean into a service that is more aligned and better appreciated?
- Should I continue or accelerate something I am already doing well?
- Should we stop something we are not doing that well? Or should we try and figure out if we can salvage it?

YOUR FROM → TO PERSONAL GOAL:

FROM being a leader who worships at the altar of self-preservation, TO being a leader focused on the bigger picture and mutual alignment with clients and internal teams.

LESSON 9

X + 1

When I have the chance to meet new employees, I always ask them two favors. The first is that they hold on to their newness as a secret weapon and be sure to help improve the company with their ideas. The second is what this chapter is about: delivering X + 1. X + 1 is a philosophy shift. It is about delivering X (what the actual request was) and then +1 (something more).

This is not a chapter about overdelivery. Overdelivery is nothing to be celebrated. Basic overdelivery simply implies you provided more than what was asked but with no indication of whether the juice was worth the squeeze. In other words, did the extra you provided actually move the needle? It's more like special delivery that matters.

How did I come to this philosophy? This insight came from

a mentor at Coca-Cola, Stuart Kronauge. I was working for Stuart on Fanta, when over the cubicle, she quickly asked me to pull case sales for Fanta TM for October 5, 2006. She had to run up to some big meeting and needed the data. So, I diligently went into the system and pulled the data and furnished the simple data point on the left, in the next chart (which is what I was asked for).

Stuart said a quick "thank you" and rushed off to her meeting. On her way back, she stopped by my desk and talked to me for a bit about what opportunity I had missed. She let me know, "You did what I asked for but did not help anticipate my need." She went on to explain and remind me that a data point is more useful in context. (Funny enough, this is what my statistics professor always reminded me of, saying, "Point estimates are for suckers.") She went on to say that case sales would have been more useful if compared by the same day, and then year over year, as well as trended by day for that week. This would then contextualize, in more richness, how Fanta actually sold on that particular day.

What I was asked for...

Case sales for Fanta™ 10/5/2006
1,000,000

What I should have delivered...

Same day YOY	Case sales for Fanta™ 10/5/2005	Case sales for Fanta™ 10/5/2006	YOY Change
	900,000	1,000,000	11%

Daily Trended	Case sales for Fanta™ 10/5/2005	Case sales for Fanta™ 10/6/2005	Case sales for Fanta™ 10/7/2005
	900,000	950,000	975,000

While this story is one I took away from my time at Coca-Cola, the lesson here translates very well to the Great Client Partner. Picture a typical scenario where the client asks you for a snapshot of results for the fourth quarter to share at their board meeting. Instead of just sharing quarterly results, be sure to compare to year-over-year fourth quarter results as well as Q1, Q2, and Q3.

The important point here, though, is that this X + 1 is the mentality to be in, and not just one that is about the presentation of data or results. A client might ask you for insights on a particular target segment, but perhaps you anticipate that it's important to compare that segment against another option, so they can see alternatives or comparable targets. Train yourself and your team to think in terms of X + 1. That being said, don't let the +1 be make-work or busywork, but rather smart, surgical, and helpful work.

While the story I just shared is about anticipating business needs, the Great Client Partner also works tirelessly to anticipate needs the client did not even know they had. These tend to be emotional needs. We forget, clients are people too. They have mortgages, they have kids, they have wives, husbands and partners, dogs, sick cousins, and neighbors whose trees have fallen on their houses. They have birthdays, celebrations, anniversaries, and promotions. They also have reorgs, mean bosses, and political landscapes.

For one of our favorite clients, we threw a huge thirtieth birthday party blowout. We had his picture transposed onto a cake and made top-ten T-shirts. For another client who loved jazz and dancing, we took her out to Lincoln Center for Dancing Under the Stars, in New York City. I remember that night very well. The client leader from our team was not much for dancing or public displays that could be embarrassing, but deep down, he really liked this client and cared about her as a person and a client. So, there he was, dancing under the stars.

For one client who recently had to lay off most of her team, we offered (at no cost) to help prop up her team for a period of time, while she dug out of the hole she was left to fill. For one client who was aiming for a very deserved promotion, we dug deep to help him get that VP promotion—and that became a rallying cry for our team. When he got the promotion, we sent him a card signed by our entire twenty-person team, and I can tell you we all felt like we got promoted that day.

The point is, getting to great requires an X + 1 mentality that covers the work and the emotion.

THREE HABIT CHANGES

1. Live X + 1. Every time you have an assignment, think about the ask, but then also about what you can do to add more depth of insight to it. Make X + 1 a mantra.
2. Make things more personal. How do you invest into a client such that you anticipate their emotional needs, not just the material needs?
3. Start to think about trust as a bank account; if you plan to make withdrawals, you have to make deposits. And if you are in the agency business, it can't be expected to be even. Understand that you should make more deposits than withdrawals.

YOUR FROM → TO PERSONAL GOAL:

FROM being a leader who merely does what is requested, TO being a leader who anticipates needs and looks over the horizon.

LESSON 10

GET ON A PLANE AND DITCH THE POWERPOINT

One August we were having some challenges with a client. We had been with them for a decade. The relationship was extremely important. In the most accidental of ways, we had gotten a bit on the back foot. I was the executive sponsor on the business, so the buck stopped at my desk. My first instinct was to rally the team and come up with a forty-slide deck to share our genius plan to evolve our marketing program. To make that deck would have taken hundreds of hours and delayed us for weeks. Instead, I realized that the bigger issue than the work was that the trust was broken. Slides were not the answer. Time, listening, and trust rebuilding was required.

Instead, I got on a plane to see the client. I went without

a PowerPoint deck. I just asked questions, gave some counsel, got some feedback, talked about the future, and tried to understand what was going on in the business. You don't always need PowerPoint slides to make progress.

How did I come to this conclusion? What made me confident enough to leave the deck behind? Ultimately, I asked myself three questions I might recommend you think about as well:

- Is the time (measured in weeks) it takes to create incredible content worth the risk that the delay causes?
- Is the issue at hand truly about the content, or is the real issue a break in trust?
- Might it be better to brainstorm with the client versus share slides (which tends to cut down conversation)?

Too many are taught too young to value a meeting by the number of slides in the presentation. The bigger the meeting, the bigger the PowerPoint deck, goes the thinking. The longer the meeting, the higher the slide count. It is something we are taught unconsciously, and it's hard to unlearn. It also creates a barrier between you getting in a car or a plane to see your clients.

I was once meeting with an account director on a retail client heading into their Q4 season and I asked him, "We are a few weeks away from Black Friday. When are you heading out to see the client next?"

He replied, "Well, we don't have any decks or presentations to give right now, so we had nothing on the books."

When I picked my jaw up off the floor, I realized he simply had equated the threshold for seeing a client to having a large PowerPoint presentation to share.

This is the shortest chapter in the book, perhaps symbolically. The only lesson here is to recognize that there are a hundred good reasons to make the trip to see your client and walk their halls. Take them to lunch, ask them how their business is doing, ask them how their family is doing, and get a feel for stress levels in their halls.

THREE HABIT CHANGES

1. Visit your clients in person whenever the chance arises.
2. Don't think of the threshold as having a large Power-Point deck but rather a multitude of reasons.
3. Understand that the value of walking the halls at the client site allows you to have a better feel for the business you are working so hard to represent.

YOUR FROM → TO PERSONAL GOAL:

FROM a leader who thinks in PowerPoint first, TO someone who trusts their own voice and instincts as reason enough to see a client and walk the halls.

PART 2

GETTING THE MOST OUT OF YOUR TEAM

LESSON 11

BE A SERVANT LEADER

"My job is to empower you all to reach your potential."
—TIM ANDREE, EXECUTIVE CHAIRMAN,
DENTSU AEGIS NETWORK

The notion of servant leadership means adopting a style of leading that puts the team first and yourself second. You should have a mental state that recognizes you hold your office as a public trust and can get voted out if you don't represent and respect those that work for you and keep you in office. Servant leadership is not a catch phrase; it should be as sacred as a religion. It is a vast subject, deserving of its own book, but let's simplify it here and just consider what it means in terms of leadership behavior.

Before jumping in, it's important to visualize what servant leadership looks like in its most simple form.

As illustrated, the notion is that, traditionally, the employee base of the company works for and takes orders from the leader(s). This is a command-and-control notion that is more effective in a military setting (though even that is changing). The servant leader illustration is one in which the leader works at the service of the employee base. To be clear, this is not to be confused with a twenty-four-year-old copywriter ordering around the CEO, but rather that the CEO views it as her job to work in the best interests and service of the copywriter. It's not semantics, it's a huge difference.

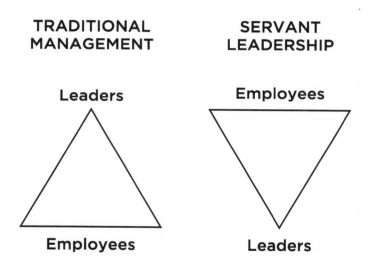

Ultimately, behaviors and actions speak louder than rhetoric and words. Accordingly, I have tried my best to outline some behaviors of a servant leader. You won't do them all right every day (I sure don't), but if you think about them and raise your level of self-awareness around them, you will be on your way toward creating a servant leadership culture, which is something that is sustainable and enduring.

- **Behaviors.** Everyone is always looking at you for signals of your management style. Everything communicates, so what do you want to communicate as a servant leader? Here are a few things to focus on from a behavior perspective.
- **Sit on the side of the table in any room.** When you enter a room and you see a long boardroom-looking table, the instinct as a leader is to sit at the head of a table. Resist it, and instead, sit at the side. This is less of a command-and-control posture and will set the room further at ease and allow everyone to contribute.
- **Put your hands on the keyboard.** If you call a Sunday meeting to get ready for a big new business pitch, don't just sit there and bark out orders for others to make the content. Ensure you grab a section. Even further, grab something unsavory and difficult, like the staffing model. Be a worker and a contributor, not just a talking head.
- **Help with the mundane things.** This is exactly what it sounds like. When the Chinese food is ordered, and you are all working late at night, and the meal is done, and you are all wondering how General Tso is going to find its way to the garbage can in the corner that is

simply too small...you be the one to step up, grab some dishes and get them in the garbage. Don't leave it to the intern or office services. Take care of it and help.

- **Be equitable with reviews.** Make sure reviews are 360 degrees in nature. This ensures that everyone feels like they get a say in the feedback that goes to your leaders. Beyond reviews, creating a culture that relishes feedback reminds people they are accountable to everyone, not just the boss.

- **Be generous at big meetings and invite the shy ones in.** Be brave yourself and make sure junior folks get involved in big meetings, so it's clear you believe in the entire team, not just your stars. This sends a message that everyone can make a vital contribution. Further, make overt efforts to bring those who are by nature more reserved into the debate by asking them questions directly. It is often the quiet ones who are sitting on some of the best ideas. Show you care about all ideas from all people, and you will receive an increased flow of great ideas.

- **Give everyone else credit and use "we" in all communications instead of "I."** This is simple. When talking, emailing, or texting, take pains to focus on the team. At first, it will feel forced, but it does wonders for team morale.

- **Don't protect senior leadership.** If you are reading this book and you have influence to make changes in the senior ranks, then take that responsibility very seriously and don't hide the flaws of senior leadership. If someone needs to be removed, then do so. If you retain a senior leader who is flawed, it tells the rest of the team that those flaws meet your standards. Twice in my career I was guilty of this, and I still regret both instances.

Servant Leadership is truly a concept that, if embraced, can become a movement in your company. It can be a snowball that becomes something huge where the office and everyone in it becomes focused on the work and never on the ego. Truly, servant leadership is the engine of any Great Client Partner.

- **DO THE LITTLE THINGS, RELIABLY.** Another part of being a servant leader is being accountable to others. And here, "others" doesn't just mean being accountable to the client or your boss, but everyone you come into contact with.* Everyone needs to believe you will do what you say and say what you do.

Do the little things, consistently. Arthur Weinbach, the former CEO of ADP Payroll, told me, "Get in there and be the first guy to plug in the coffee pot." While sitting on a patio outside his home, Arthur related to me the story

---

* For more on this subject, I recommend one of my favorite account books, entitled *The Trusted Advisor*, written by David Maister (along with Charles H. Green and Robert M. Galford). Reliability is a key concept.

of how, when he was a young accountant, he would come in early every single day and plug in the coffee pot. It was not a huge thing, but it was a gesture. It showed he was in bright and early and that he was the indispensable person who set the day in motion.

Arthur did this every day. It became a habit. Little things turn into big things. Little good habits turn into big habits and bigger momentum.

I see this play out all the time in account management, but sometimes it's a silent killer. There was someone who used to work for me, who we will call Jim. Jim serviced one of our most important and largest accounts at our agency. Jim was a fantastic client leader in most regards, but he very often was late on the delivery of his weekly report to the client. Each week, it seemed, there was a different reason and excuse. Compared to all the great things Jim was doing in terms of strategy and revenue delivery, this seemed like a very small thing to Jim. However, what was happening was that tardiness eroded the client's overall trust in him. Jim just did not believe that the little things mattered. He did not understand that he was eroding his own reliability. Ultimately, Jim was moved off the account, which also hurt his standing internally within the agency. Jim came to understand that not doing the little things can erode the faith people have in you even if you are great at the bigger things.

DO-TO-SAY RATIO

Adam Bryant, author of *The Corner Office*, offered one of my favorite statements during the course of a CEO interview. He noted that he looks at leaders by evaluating their "do-to-say ratio." As a leader, the most important thing for you to do in terms of increasing your reliability is to maintain a high do-to-say ratio. It is a signpost of a great servant leadership culture when people honor their promises to each other, not out of fear but because the culture demands it. This is not because you don't want to let down the bosses but rather because you don't want to let down each other. Finally, the leaders will ensure they honor their promises because they don't want to let down those they serve.

It's very easy to make promises like, "I am on it," "I got this," or the dreaded, "No problem. You will have it tomorrow." The issue is that even though you might forget your promise, thinking perhaps that it was a small task and it didn't mean anything, others remember and lose faith in you.

Make promises, sign up for deadlines, be clear on deliverables—and then actually hit those deadlines. If you need to be late, telegraph that early.

THREE HABIT CHANGES

1. Do-to-say ratio—keep a record of your promises. If complex, do it via shortcuts such as loading your calendar with meetings that are essentially critical reminders, or even your iPhone memo app. But keep a promise log, and then keep your promises.

2. Plug in the coffee machine—and by that, I mean, find your own small contribution and make it matter. Bring coffee to meetings you host. Print clean agendas on crisp paper each time.

3. Make a list of your most common behaviors as a leader—just the first habits that pop into your head. Do these exemplify servant leadership? Why or why not?

YOUR FROM → TO PERSONAL GOAL:

FROM being a leader who thinks their organization works for them, TO being a leader who wakes up every day trying to serve those around you and make them better.

LESSON 12

GIVE FACTUAL FEEDBACK TO EXPERTS

"Don't tell creatives that it's easy to just turn a 6 into a 9."

—DIAHANN YOUNG, DIRECTOR OF DIGITAL
PLATFORMS AND INNOVATION AT PULTEGROUP

Great Client Partners have to give feedback to great subject matter experts. They could be technical experts, creative experts, analytics experts, or really, subject matter experts of any sort—but whatever their role, they'll have more expertise in their domain than the client leader or the client. Being able to convey feedback well, whether it's your own perspective or that of the client, whether it's a glowing review or constructive criticism, will make or break you, and by extension, your team.

So the first thing to do is get comfortable with the fact that your value is in the synthesis, the filtering, and the nuance of how you deliver the feedback. Convey feedback poorly, and you lose the team. Do it right, and you are on track to be CEO—or at least, certainly, a Great Client Partner.

As I learned from Vipul Kapadia, the founder of ThinqShift, a good friend, and a change management guru, there are three types of power, each of which colors feedback delivery. They are content, positional, and personal power.

- *Content*—This type of power and influence is derived from your expertise and what you know. For a client leader, this is not media, analytics, or engineering. This is the knowledge you have about the client, their business, and their politics. Leaders must recognize that content power is knowledge, not just a skill.
- *Positional*—This is the type of power you have over those who report to you. It's a power type with a lot of impact, but it can easily be abused. It's the least powerful of the superpowers because in most situations, 80 percent of the team does not report to you.
- *Personal*—This power is derived from your relationships. Who wants to go the extra mile for you? It's Friday, and you need your team to work the weekend to get the result that is required to win. If you have true personal power here, the team rallies and is excited to

get to work. If you don't have it, you hear excuses about their uncle's birthday or the bris they must attend.

It's critical to give feedback to SMEs using your personal power first, plus a bit of your content power (but only as it relates to your knowledge of the client and their business). Client leaders often complain that "it's impossible to give feedback to the VP of analytics because he does not report to me." But your ability to influence people with indirect power will likely define how successful you are at your job, so think about how to use these types of power to relate effectively to people who do not report to you—people like that VP of analytics.

At our agency, looking at ten years of data, I can tell you that individuals who are the most indispensable, the most highly compensated, and the most influential are those who are the best at having difficult conversations.

If you can follow these five simple golden rules of giving feedback to experts on your team, you will be an account person for the ages.

FIVE GOLDEN EXPERT FEEDBACK RULES

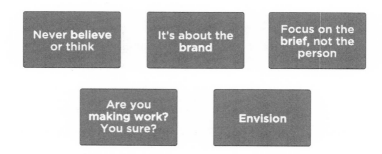

NEVER BELIEVE OR THINK—ALWAYS MAKE IT ABOUT FACTS.

Context: As a client leader, your influence, power, leverage, and usefulness come from your knowledge and your access to the client. You should write this down, say it in your daily affirmation, and commit it to memory. It's the most profound and humbling thing I can explain in this book. If information is power (the good kind, not the *Star Wars III* type where Anakin goes all crazy), then client leaders derive their power from the information they get most directly from the clients. How you wield that power defines your ability to be great. To be clear, the only way to put that power to use is to make the work, and the team, better—not to lord over folks that you know something they don't know.

In other words, it is more powerful to relay facts than conjecture.

When I was coming up through the ranks, I worked for a client leader who was very talented, but she often started delivering bad news by saying, "Folks, we need to work late tonight to redo the deck, because I just don't *think* we have enough of an analytical bent to it...it just *feels* like we need more math and quant in there." This always killed me inside. Had she started off by saying, "I just got some direct feedback from the client who expressed that they expect to see a ton of analysis behind each recommendation at tomorrow's meeting," then my desire to pitch in would have gone up tenfold. This subtle difference in wielding fact versus feeling can put power into each sentence you utter as a client leader.

Consider: The quickest way to annoy a SME is to start a sentence by saying "I think" or "I believe." No team member wants to hear your opinion as though you're the pope. While it is actually very good for you to have thoughts that lead (i.e., original ideas that move a client, industry, or team forward), beginning a sentence with "I believe" suggests your thoughts come from your gut, not your brain, and certainly not from your discussion with a client. Belief or feeling also makes it hard to distinguish your opinion from the factual information that is being relayed about what the client directly said.

Tip: Try communicating with specifics instead, such as:

- "Jason, your work was great. The issue is the client has realized the margin gained on children's dress clothes are superior to that of designer women's clothing. Your work was thoughtful, but they are going in a new direction. I hate those facts as much as you do, but that is our new arena of battle."
- "Tameka, our client has asked that we put to the side the more youthful concept and focus 100 percent of the team's energy on the designer looks with two new versions within ten business days."
- "The work you just produced is awesome, but based on the client's new focus, we should consider a slight repositioning to align with that. Here are the two core elements to use as a filter based on the client's recent briefing of their new direction."

As you can see, in both role-plays, separating out fact delivery from opinion delivery is key. In addition, showing that you also feel the frustration will mean you get better at demonstrating empathy, which is a core trait of any Great Client Partner.

IT'S ALWAYS ABOUT THE BRAND.

Context: The client leader should know more about the brand than anyone else. That is the core of your influence and expertise. The client leader should understand the history of the brand, the rules, the laws, IP issues, competitive issues, color choices, sacred cows, internal politics, and more. Use this knowledge for good; it is your North Star.

Fact: If you find yourself saying, "That is too yellow," or, "That copy has no hook," or, "Those keywords will never work," or, "Those graphs just don't grab my attention," or, "Why is this deck so darned long?" count to ten and try a new way because you are failing yourself and your team.

Tip: Try these responses instead:

- "That tagline does not highlight or maximize the brand Reasons to Believe (RTB)."
- "That analysis was very cool, but I am afraid it won't answer the current brand problem of margin loss that this client is dealing with."
- "I wish we could experiment with all those keywords you have suggested, but the brand guidelines run counter to that. How do you suggest we bridge that gap?"
- "I wish we could get in all those graphs and exhibits you created, but we need to remember this client has a custom that decks should be no more than ten pages. Let's work to adapt to their brand of information review."

In short, make it about the client's brand and the client's

style—so use specifics to describe potential issues—and never attack the person, which leads to the next principle.

FOCUS ON THE BRIEF AND THE CHALLENGE, NOT THE PERSON.

Context: Teams often take a lot of time to settle on a brief. The brief in the marketing services business is meant to be both a compact and a North Star. It is meant to be a short summary of what you are trying to achieve with a given campaign or initiative and then what has been agreed upon between client and agency. However, we often see a situation where all the parties spend days on landing a brief but then fail to use it as a true North Star. When this happens, situations devolve into commentary about individuals on the team.

Fact: SMEs need to remember where their work leads to. When work goes off the rails, re-share the physical brief/email/stimuli and just circle the relevant part. Take the personal out of it and focus the debate on the brief and away from the person.

Tip: Try these responses instead:

- "The brief we agreed to had 'value' as a key construct, yet 80 percent of this ad copy does not mention price or value. Can you help me understand how you see your work landing the 'value' element of the brief?"

- "We agreed as a team to make conversion yield a focus this quarter, yet 85 percent of the ideas on the list are about brand awareness. The brief we are all working from, approved by the client, really demands our focus be on conversion, not awareness...fair?"

ENVISION

Context: Your role as a leader is to help your team see a vision for a better tomorrow. They need to see how you see the account being run a year from now. Are you producing better work as a team and tackling meatier assignments? If so, how do you propose to actualize them? Just like in politics, if you don't show a vision, then others will imagine one that is inferior and at best distracting to the real mission.

So envision for the good of your team.

Fact: If there is nothing to envision, and no North Star guiding you, then your team is not working toward anything specific or unifying. This might mean the team is not working passionately.

Tip: At the start of every year's planning, have a North Star meeting. This is your opportunity to shine as the

Great Client Partner. It's where you help folks see where the brand and the remit can go. How do you propose to move the relationship to be exponentially bigger, global in nature, and retained in terms of resources?

ARE YOU MAKING WORK?

Context: SMEs get frustrated when they perceive that a client leader is making work by ignoring the 80/20 principle. A Great Client Partner will work hard to make sure their team is doing the work needed to win and not a single minute more. A brilliant client leader will work to make sure the SME is on the phone or in the room when the client ask comes in, so that (1) they can hear it directly and (2) they can feel the accountability of hearing a request firsthand.

Fact: Make sure you are always driving revisions/improvements based on client needs, not your own worries or your own fear. Account people who make work for the team but don't understand the difference between "essential" and "important" can never lead for a sustained period of time.

Tip: Try saying this (for example, to your analytics partner on the team):

I know this is a third revision, but the last forecast did not account for seasonality, which called into question the rigor of our forecast. As a team, we can't let that happen, or it will mean diminished stature in the client's eyes for years to come. This is a critical business item, folks.

THREE HABIT CHANGES

1. In your feedback delivery, practice focusing on the specific factors relevant to your client. Get used to referring to your brief and the client's mission instead of calling out a team member or stating your opinion.
2. Take time out of your workweek and jot down a North Star that you can guide your team by. Envision where you want to go and how you'll get there and put something on paper. It doesn't matter how fully fledged the idea is at this point. The important thing is that you're thinking about it and moving toward it.
3. Eliminate "I feel" and "I think" from your feedback vocabulary.

YOUR FROM → TO PERSONAL GOAL:

FROM being a leader who gives feedback from a "feeling" perspective, TO a leader who gives feedback via objective, fact-driven vantage points.

LESSON 13

RUN THE MEETING. DON'T LET MEETINGS RUN YOU.

Meetings are the worst sin in the advertising and marketing services world. On any given week, 10 to 50 percent of an employee's time is spent in meetings. They are very expensive, often poorly run, and tend to create a lot of frustration. A Great Client Partner runs a great meeting. There is nothing natural about knowing how to run a great meeting, so please consider the following steps.

1. **Clear Agenda, Distributed in Advance.** The best meetings have agendas. Agendas do not need to be complicated, but they should list the top three goals of the meeting in a prioritized order. For example, an agenda for your weekly status on a typical account might look like this:

- ◦ Review past week's campaign results—How were the results last week?
- ◦ Focus on hurdles and how to get over them—What is blocking us from success?
- ◦ Team check-in—How are the core team members doing?

(Note that this agenda is neither too specific [confining] nor too vague [wasteful and rudderless.])

2. **Well-chosen attendance list.** A lazy, weekly status meeting that runs for an hour can cost north of $1,000 in billable time. That is time theft. The Great Client Partner will be polite, yet ruthless about the attendance list. The notion is to include only those who will contribute or who need to hear the information directly to do their job. Resist the notion to include folks in your meeting so they stay in the loop. As a golden rule, also look to avoid duplication. If you have a media supervisor in the meeting, then it is not typically critical to invite a media manager or media director. Have that one representative share the information if possible.

3. **Announce the purpose of the meeting at the start, as a ritual.** A small ritual that can go a long way is to start each meeting by announcing the purpose. This provides orientation. Literally say, "Thank you all for being here. The purpose of this meeting is to align before we visit the client in Florida this Friday."

4. **Time.** Let me say something controversial here. You should have no more than one single hour-long meeting per week. Let that be your most important, debate-driven meeting, but beyond that, most of your meetings should be thirty minutes in duration. The issue is that when a meeting is an hour, it provides no reason to be concise and organized. A thirty-minute meeting puts the emphasis on preparation.

5. **Cut off distractions, but kindly.** If your thirty-minute meeting's stated purpose is "to determine the casting for the upcoming new business pitch," then it is not acceptable for someone to take you down a tangent around pricing. Tangents are natural. However, nature is not an excuse. Be better and avoid tangents.

6. **Take a shy inventory.** As mentioned in Lesson 11 (Servant Leadership), some of the best team members with some of the best ideas might just be painfully shy or uncertain of themselves. In a meeting, what tends to happen is that similar people's voices get heard, and as a result, the best ideas do not come to the surface. Your job as the leader of the meeting is to find a way that the best ideas get heard. As you move through the meeting, do your best to take a mental inventory. If Sally, who is shy but skillful and insightful, has not yet chimed in, call on her and ask her to volunteer her thoughts. She will first want to stab you, but then will talk, and others will realize you are the type of leader who wants to hear from the many.

7. **Use meetings to debate, not to inform (ideally).** When I was in my early twenties, I used to think meetings were a time where I got to show off my wisdom and chops in front of eight or so of my coworkers. When I got to 360i, Bryan Wiener would often advocate that I send the deck or pre-work twenty-four hours before. His rationale was that a meeting should be about debate, and that everyone should already have the information prior to the meeting. If the first fifteen minutes of your meeting is to level-set, then 50 percent of your time, at best, is now available for problem-solving and debate. Insist on information being sent out twenty-four hours in advance of the meeting with an email:

Tom, please prepare a two-sheeter for everyone around churn stats by account, trended by month, and send to this invitee group twenty-four hours before the meeting so we can make it as productive as possible.

8. **Next Steps and Follow Up.** Follow up. Make your follow-up timely, simple, bulleted, and ensure that each bullet has a date, owner, and deliverable.

THREE HABIT CHANGES

1. Review the points listed in this chapter before you schedule your next few meetings. Review them over and over until they are second nature.

2. Take a minute to talk to your colleagues about how they run their meetings. They might have some great ideas specific to your department.

3. Spend some quiet time looking over the roster of your meetings and think about how you expect (and hope) each team member will contribute.

YOUR FROM → TO PERSONAL GOAL:

FROM having runaway meetings, TO running meetings efficiently and effectively.

LESSON 14

SEE THE MEETING WITHIN THE MEETING

"Jared, I think we were in two different meetings."

—JIM WARNER, FORMER PRESIDENT OF
RAZORFISH AND CBS NETWORKS

Not too long ago, I was involved with a great team pitch for a major US retailer. Things were going exactly as planned. We had performed our introductions as scripted. We got through the credentials slides flawlessly, just as practiced. Each team member was getting up one after the next to take the prospective client through their expertise. One spoke nearly perfectly about search, while another talked about social media, and the last spoke about analytics. Each person was great. The majority of those on my team seemed pleased with how the meeting was going.

I was horrified.

Why was there such a difference in how we were perceiving the same meeting?

Simple. My teammates were focused on what was being presented, while I was focused on the faces of those receiving the information, the clients. By my measure, the faces of the clients each were a bit sullen and disinterested. They were polite looks. They were looking at our slides but were not engaged in them. I glanced at my watch and noticed we were averaging twenty minutes between any client question or interruption. The senior client had not been heard from since her introduction at the start of the meeting. In short, we were running a meeting, but the client was not with us.

At this point, I politely raised my hand, stood up, and said, "Let's pause the meeting for a minute. These two hours are about you, not us, and we are not hearing enough from you in terms of your needs, your concerns, your worries, or your hopes. Let's talk about those for twenty minutes, and then we can focus on areas of our prepared material that best maps to those needs."

The client was surprised, but that soon turned to absolute joy. One of my partners grabbed a marker and worked the whiteboard while I played host. We had an enthusiastic twenty-minute session where we listed and categorized the client's needs. From there, we created a bit of a choose-your-own-adventure methodology for the rest of the meeting. The meeting was a success in the end, and we went on to win the business.

The Great Client Partner is reading the signals the client is putting out there, be they verbal or nonverbal, obvious or obscure. The Great Client Partner often leaves a meeting with a totally different accounting of how that meeting went than anyone else who was in the room.

When I was in my early twenties, I was on the road while working at Avenue A with the president of our agency at the time, Jim Warner. We were spending time with a then up-and-coming job search site called jobsdirect.com. We were presenting to the CMO about our plans to drive revenue for their site and help them achieve their ambitions. We got in the car, and Jim asked me how the meeting went.

With the confidence associated with someone in their twenties, I said, "I thought it was a home run. We got through our content really well, and on time."

Then I asked Jim for his two cents. Needless to say, he thought it was a poor meeting. "The client spoke for only 10 percent of the time," he recounted. "The client asked only four questions. The client offered no buy-in signals that we were on the same page. The client was distracted in a number of ways."

He leaned back in the car as we headed back to the office and said, "Jared, I think we were in two different meetings." Jim was never rude; he was simply trying to underscore a point. That point is that the success of each meeting hinges on reading the room in a level of depth that most folks don't focus on.

One of the ways to get better at reading a room and looking for nonverbal clues is by getting into the habit of evaluation. If you know what to look for and have your own checklist of questions, then you will eventually do this naturally. For now, here is a cheat sheet of sorts that might help you better understand how the client meeting you are hosting is really going.

WHAT DO YOU SEE?

Are your clients taking notes? Or are they distracted?

Are your clients smiling? Frowning? Bored?

Are your clients asking questions? Or checked out?

Did someone's body perk up on a certain piece of content?

WHAT DO YOU HEAR?

Are your clients giving you indications you missed the mark?

Are your clients building on your ideas?

Are your clients using next-steps language?

Are you hearing blocking language?

WHAT DO YOU NOT HEAR?

Are you hearing any excitement?

Are you hearing any buy-in signals?

Are you hearing trust?

Why are they not building on your ideas?

THREE HABIT CHANGES

1. Focus less on getting through a meeting and more on how the actual meeting is going by looking at non-verbal cues. Look for client comfort and interaction.
2. Don't be afraid to go off script. This is not a Broadway show.
3. Ensure that someone on the team has it as their job

to read the room while busy presenters are dealing with the content.

YOUR FROM → TO PERSONAL GOAL:

FROM a leader who thinks every meeting is great, TO a leader who identifies greatness as client engagement and has the tools to judge this accurately.

LESSON 15

CASTING

"Just put a bow tie on me and point me in the right direction."
—ELI KAUFMAN, SEM SUPERVISOR 3601

If you think about every great movie you have seen, you'll realize it was driven by a script and actors. Not only does the actor need to be great, with a great script to work from, but it has to be the right actor. Who else could have played Han Solo but Harrison Ford? As the client leader, you are the George Lucas in your little world. You have the power and privilege to put the right people in front of the right people at the right time with the right script.

There are tons of moments when casting comes into play, but for the purposes of this lesson, let's focus on two situations: the pitch and the big meeting.

CASTING FOR THE PITCH

Your most important role as a Great Client Partner is casting. Don't let your hang-ups or anxieties prevent you from being creative in your thinking. The right person for the situation might be a curious choice to others who don't know the details of the work, the client, the setting, or the situation.

I recall a situation in which we were going into a meeting to win a large piece of Search and Analytics business. The client was very quantitative in nature, so we knew bringing five new business development suits to the pitch would be a death knell. Instead, we brought Eli Kaufman, one of our most amazing SEM minds but also a unique character (as he would tell you himself). We positioned Eli as the mad scientist of SEM. We did, as he requested, give him a bow tie to wear, and we set him up in his role. We won the pitch. Later that month, when the chairman of the company called me to tell me we won, he said, "Jared, we love your agency, but we think Eli is the key to our success—that mad scientist is just what we need."

It's all about casting. A great account manager puts the right person in the right role at the right time and in the right situation. I recommend that every client leader ask themselves three core questions before deciding on a final casting recommendation.

Who is the throat to choke? Clients need to figure out who is in charge very quickly in a pitch. Who would be their person? Who will be their visionary and their day-to-day leader who pushes them forward? This can't be vague. This can't be some mash-up of a talented senior designer, a passionate CEO, and a project manager. It has to be one person. Here are some actions to take:

- *Be very clear about who the leader is.* Name this person at the start of the meeting and be consistent with these remarks throughout the pitch.
- *Be very purposeful to make that leader at least 50 percent dedicated in the staffing model.* When you have the obligation to fill out the staffing chart, be clear that the person you established as the leader at 50 percent is an allocated full-time employee or more. If you took the pain to call the person the leader only to staff them at 20 percent, you are being accidentally hypocritical. With 20 percent focus, it's hard to be very focused. What I mean here is that in an organizational chart or Excel grid, 20 percent allocation might look fine. However, 20 percent focus is not enough to move the needle for the lead on a piece of business.

Did you put feelings ahead of the win? The Great Client Partner has to put their team in the position to win and succeed for both the agency and client alike. This means that no casting decision should start with "I really feel that Sally should attend this big meeting because it's critical to her morale!" This is a dangerous statement for a principled leader to make. On the surface, this feels very human and compassionate, but it actually is selfish. It puts the feelings of one team member ahead of the win for the larger team or the best outcome for the client. The leader must put the best possible team forward and not be afraid to hurt feelings on occasion. The best presenters should present, period.

Did you over include people at the expense of intimacy? Cast for intimacy. Intimacy in this usage is about ensuring the room does not get too big. In the agency world, there is a gravitational pull to over include. It happens for good reasons, but it can be counterproductive. What typically happens is the account person decides he needs the quant, the creative, the search specialist, the AI guy, and the experienced design expert. Each invite seems like it will add value in an expert-driven society. However, what seems to happen is that too many people talk too few net moments, and there is no connection, no intimacy in the room. My recommendation is there should be no more than five to eight people in a room for a big moment or pitch.

CASTING FOR THE "BIG MEETING"

While the pitch may only happen once or twice a year, the big meeting is far more common in the everyday work world and will partially define your reputation as a Great Client Partner. So consider these elements:

- Intimacy—Some of the best "big meetings" were small meetings. I once brought just the lead account person, a strategist, and the head of analytics to a big meeting with a large client and found this led to a greater level of intimacy in the room. People share more in small settings. Any more than five people in a room guarantees less truth sharing.
- Expertise—Bring expertise that is unexpected. If your clients know more than you do, you are not adding enough value to earn a premium.
- North Star—Every great meeting should start with a simple reflection: "What is our North Star?" Identify what you are trying to achieve. Then it should be written up on the whiteboard in the room.

Whether it's a big meeting or a pitch meeting, be sure to align on what you want to accomplish. The one thing I always remember is what my old boss, Jason Trevisan, told me. "Clients are rarely both surprised and delighted at the same time."

What did he mean by this? Well, advertising and marketing folks love the surprise. By this, I mean that marketing and services folks alike love the grand reveal and the high that comes from unveiling some new innovation, idea, or campaign. They love to build up tension and then pay it off with some grand ending and solution. This is an unnecessary challenge, however. If you are too good at creating the tension, you need to be even better at selling the solution in order to get past the distraction caused by the presentation.

Instead, the best two things to do are: (1) align the meeting with the client or prospect, making sure you both know and agree on what needs to be accomplished, and (2) tell them what you are going to tell them, tell them, and tell them what you told them. This is the classic rule for presentations, both for pitches and the big meeting.

THREE HABIT CHANGES

1. In the next meeting you are running, take a body language inventory and pay attention to what the client is doing, what their faces look like, and how they're holding themselves. To maximize engagement, take risks of casting, but make sure everyone is set up for success and has a very specific role.

2. Avoid the grand reveal and bring clients along with your work and thinking. Avoid the surprise and delight mentality.

3. Be the master by focusing on casting to win, not casting for morale wins.

YOUR FROM → TO PERSONAL GOAL:

FROM a leader who thinks only about the content of the pitch or big meeting, TO someone who obsesses about the characters in the meeting.

LESSON 16

NOT EVERYTHING IS A FIRE

"Use a pencil instead of a space pen whenever you can."

—KEVIN GERAGHTY, VP, DATA ANALYTICS
AT AVALONBAY COMMUNITIES

The 80/20 rule, as it is most commonly known, is actually shorthand for an existing and well-documented concept called the Pareto Principle (see the diagram below). It is the idea that 20 percent of the effort can get you 80 percent of the results.

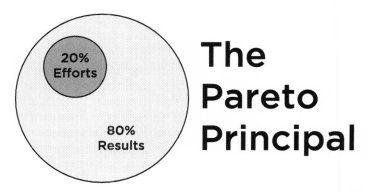

20% Efforts

80% Results

The Pareto Principal

People are perhaps more familiar with looking at this like you can get to 80 percent of the right answer and that, often, it's not worth the extra effort to get to 90 percent or 100 percent. The notion being that, in many situations, 80 percent is good enough and that it's time to move on.

Of course, this is not always the case. One of my oldest and best friends, Jordan Schecter, is in oncology. I would think his patients would all agree that 100 percent accuracy is damned important. Alas, for us folks in the services business, we tend not to deal in life and death scenarios like he does, so 80 percent is often a golden rule. It's about harnessing efficiency and productivity for the best outcomes.

Having a good grasp of the 80/20 rule is a great thing because it allows you to know how to prioritize your tasks. Too often, client leaders seek perfection, which can be counterproductive. In seeking perfection, client leaders also tend to see fires where in fact there is only smoke or even just a bit of heat.

A great story that brings this 80/20 rule to light is that of the space race between Russia and the United States. This was a very heated and competitive time for both nations. While the US was doing very well in its conquest of space, there were always new obstacles to overcome. One such famous example is that ballpoint pens didn't work in the absence of a gravitational pull. American scientists dealt with this by spending a reported $12 million inventing a new pen that could write upside down. For such a small instrument, the thing was a scientific marvel, solving all the problems introduced by the twentieth-century environment. Meanwhile, the Russians also came up with a solution—they used a pencil. It was free and elegant. The space pen, meanwhile, can be bought for a few dollars at the Smithsonian gift shop. The Great Client Partner thinks about the pencil solution before jumping to the pen solution.

A Great Client Partner has to figure out how to use 80/20 thinking to avoid creating a nonsustainable, reactive, driven team of firefighters instead of thinkers. You have to calibrate a filter that is an ongoing, human cost-benefit analysis tabulation. It's not about what you could do, but rather what you should do, all related to what else you now can't do as a result of this new thing you actually do.

The issue is that, all too often, due to stress and time issues, we just run from fire to fire. Your credibility as an account person hinges on your Accurate Fire Prediction Ratio (AFPR—a keenly important term I just invented—don't fret if you can't find it on Google yet).

Your AFPR is a simple equation: the number of times you yell *fire* divided by the number of actual fires that are verified and believed to be fires by your team and clients.

If your ratio falls too high, your credibility will be flushed, and you will not be able to move your team forward. Your earliest learning of this AFPR concept is the childhood story of the boy who cried wolf. It's a universal lesson yet so hard for so many to adhere to.

There are common situations that can tempt your AFPR into the danger zone. However, if you apply the 80/20 rule to these common situations, you can be a hero. Let's discuss perhaps the most classic and frequent AFPR ruiner of all time. We'll call it "The Good Deck vs. the Perfect Deck."

In most cases, a deck that you have to create for a client will be seen for twenty minutes and then never thought of again. Listeners remember your words more often than slides or remember even just a feeling based on your actions. Your job as the account lead is to ensure that the deck plays its role in being a communication aide. Your other job, based on that, is to know when good is good enough. If it's 10:00 p.m. the night before a presentation, and you have your team perfecting slides instead of focusing on chemistry, practice, and delivery, then you are violating the 80/20 rule and have scored a very low AFPR.

Over time, you should get good enough to run a simple lens through your head. However, in the early days, I would recommend a simple chart to help keep your AFPR high and the trust in your leadership skills high. Consider this simple rubric:

Task	What is really at stake?	What grade does the task require?	Does the client ever notice perfect execution on this?	What are the odds of a B hurting the outcome?	How many hours should I invest?
Present at a meeting	The client could be expecting greater detail	B+	Rarely	10%	50

The only wrong rubric is to go with your emotions and have no rubric at all. The true key is to use some type of hard metrics, so you are not tempted to use your gut.

So that is the lens for the first part of the challenge to Great Client Partners—knowing how to prioritize tasks. It should help you think of how to mitigate problems.

But let's get to the more interesting part. How do you think more structurally about when to go for it and get your team to rally around you—to really go all the way and believe in the pitch, the cause, the campaign, and the work you need them to do?

Great Client Partners earn the belief of their team and their clients based on a combination of a few things: (1) the reasons and justification provided for this belief; (2)

the likelihood, or odds, of a good outcome; (3) the level of desirability of that outcome in the first place—and all that is divided against the costs associated with pursuing that belief, whether it's a financial cost or other resources.

A simple prioritization grid like the one below is very simple and always in fashion. It simply allows you to put forth three priorities, the associated investment request, and the thought of outcome, in ordered fashion. Clear, simple, and easy to use in any situation.

OPPORTUNITY	DESCRIPTION	INVESTMENT REQUEST	PROJECTED OUTCOME, TIMING, PROBABILITY
A	Upgrade senior analytics capability on team	Additional $20K in salary investment to upgrade resource	High impact: client will appreciate the expertise, resulting in expanded analytics remit and 30% increase in project scope
B	Lobby to get CRM and Ad-tech help for the upcoming quarterly business review	100 hours of a CRM expert	Earn the trust in the CRM space, which is increasingly important to the client
C	Request that the chairman of the agency travel to visit the client	Time, flight, and date for chairman to visit client	Goodwill

Create and use lenses and rubrics to fully understand the multiple demands and outcomes inherent in each challenge.

THREE HABIT CHANGES

1. Use some type of lens or chart to really analyze what is at stake and to determine how much to invest. Apply math and odds to determine what is truly at risk before determining the appropriate investment into the work.
2. Carefully consider what you know about your client and their specific personalities when evaluating each task in a project.
3. Ask your team and yourself to think in terms of the 80/20 rule.

YOUR FROM → TO PERSONAL GOAL:

FROM a leader that is always in fire-drill mode, TO a leader that judiciously decides when to light a fire.

LESSON 17

HELP PEOPLE FIND THEIR SUPERPOWER, THEN ACCENTUATE IT

"Everyone has a superpower."

—KEMBREL JONES, DEPUTY VICE DEAN, THE WHARTON SCHOOL, UNIVERSITY OF PENNSYLVANNIA

Client service organizations tend to emphasize the negative in employee reviews. Don't follow that path. Great leaders realize there is more leverage in accentuating the great. Every person you lead has a superpower, some signature strength, that makes them amazing. It's your job to figure out what that superpower is and nurture it and get optimal value from it.

MEET BILLY

He is the account supervisor on your team, and he proudly works for you. He is twenty-seven years old and talented. He very badly wants to get promoted. He is enthusiastic, smart, and has real potential. Like any young employee, he has some strengths, but also has some weaknesses.

Let's assume that Billy is really strong in his skills of persuasion. On a typical one-to-ten scale, let's give him a score of eight. He is charismatic and an excellent presenter. It's clear to you and the leadership that if that skill of persuasion was nourished, it could be a major value-driver for the organization, the client, and Billy himself.

But what folks rarely stop to do is pause and ask themselves a key question: how valuable is this strength that Billy has? We rush to assign a value on the classic one-to-ten scale, but we rarely dwell on the significance of that numerical assignment and how, as a leader of men and women, you really do need to understand it because it shapes your understanding of your team and, ultimately, your team members' understanding of themselves.

If you use the first chart below (Exhibit A, the Unit Value chart), you can see that the numbers assigned take on a nonlinear, almost exponential form to them. To be clear, these values I have assigned are for illustrative purposes and are meant to convey simply that as someone gains more expertise, the value they in turn produce increases exponentially (rapidly and scales) in step-change fashion, not just in small increments. This is why someone who is a ten when it comes to presentation skills is not simply two times more valuable than a five but rather five times more valuable. What it means, for example, is that if you can get him from an eight to a nine—from great to greater—you will create and drive twenty units of value for the organization. For Billy, getting him from an eight to a nine will not be easy, but it's very possible and within his constitution and abilities to achieve it. Furthermore, that move from an eight to a nine creates massive value to your team and organization.

Now, let's assume Billy is a mere four in organizational skills. His call notes are solid, but not always delivered on time. He occasionally needs a reminder or two on random assignments. If you as his manager can get him to a five, you will only score an incremental ten points of value for your organization. And let's face it, it will be much more difficult and take dramatically more time than getting his presentation skills to a nine. For Billy, focusing on his organization shortcomings would be going against the grain.

So why all this math and curve illustration? The point is to show you that it's important to be probabilistic in how you evaluate talent. Take yourself out of the *feel* business and replace it with a more balanced approach. When you reevaluate Billy through a more math-based lens, it's very clear that getting him from an eight to a nine is the single best investment you can make, accentuating his superpowers.

EXHIBIT A: UNIT VALUE CHART	
Rank	Unit Value
1	2
2	5
3	10
4	15
5	20
6	25
7	30
8	40
9	60
10	100

Here the table is represented by this nonlinear (exponential) curve:

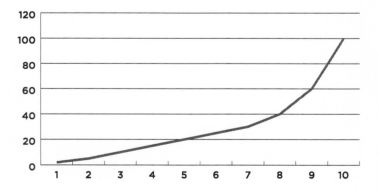

Given this, why do reviews among account people always, always focus on the negative, regardless of the value of improvement? First, there is a human instinct to manage by highlighting an employee's deficits. Second, people in general, and specifically client leaders, tend to appeal to the heart first and the math second, or last, or never.

If you apply some basic math to this logic, you can see that managing to the strengths is better. This is not to say you shouldn't address areas of development, but rather think of it as risk mitigation, not elimination. Besides accentuating the strengths, it is also important to recognize attributes that are culturally important and contagious to the interpersonal dynamics of your team, which is particularly important for client leaders.

THREE HABIT CHANGES

1. Embark on every review with empathy and identify your team members' signature strengths, their superpowers.
2. Set a course to get employees from an eight to a ten because this is where the real value lies.
3. Mitigate their weaknesses and focus on minimizing the downside of a negative trait rather than making that the focus and obsession of the review.

YOUR FROM → TO PERSONAL GOAL:

FROM a leader who harps only on the negative, TO a leader that looks for superpowers in those around you and leans into those.

LESSON 18

ENTHUSIASM AND OPTIMISM ARE WEAPONS

"Enthusiasm will be a big asset to you in your career."

—JIM WARNER, FORMER PRESIDENT OF
RAZORFISH AND CBS NETWORKS

Jim Warner, president of Avenue A at the time, decided to give me an audience. It was one of my more important reviews. He leaned back, sighed, and said, "Jared, your enthusiasm will be a big asset to you in your career, even if you create a wake of destruction with the other things you are not that great at."

It took me a minute to compute. Was this a compliment or an insult? Neither or both? What it was, ultimately, was a lesson. The observation was made, to be clear, at the highest of levels, given that Jim was the president. It struck me, accordingly, that this was a compliment. He was not calling me stupid or vapid or incapable of math. Instead, he was just saying that my best trait, the one I could most leverage, was enthusiasm and optimism.

In preparation for this book, I read over my old employee reviews. There were some good memories in there but also some hard truths to sift through. I think I began to see clearly that I was at my best when I had a manager who appreciated my ability to create revenue, to innovate, and to solve problems without harping on the little things that mattered less. It was an affirming experience because I realize more fully that my superpowers are, essentially, optimism and my ability to evangelize, to get others to believe as well.

I found one review from my time on the Fanta brand team, right out of my MBA program at Emory. The author of this review has gone on to the top of the Coca-Cola Company. She understood the importance of enthusiasm and a good attitude and took care to: (1) point it out; and (2) make sure others saw it as important.

In the forward of this book, I discussed the notion of soft skills and how these are often downplayed or worse, dismissed. In the services industry, enthusiasm is not a soft skill; it's an indispensable skill. For many clients, it's more important to know how enthusiastic and passionate your agency is about their brand or product compared to simply how knowledgeable you are about the marketing world.

Why are optimism and enthusiasm so important? In the marketing services industry, your emotional bank account is constantly debited. Long nights take their toll and are a debit. Compressed deadlines are a debit. Certain client situations can be tough, especially under stress, and those are a debit. Those debits on the emotional bank account add up. Collectively, they drain your team and can threaten the work product over time. A great leader must have followers, and followers look for enthusiasm and optimism as signposts. Further, enthusiasm and optimism are credits back into the emotional bank account of the team.

Why else? Optimism is your best and most consistent weapon to deal with the pace of change. The marketing industry is on what looks to be a multidecade radical transformation. As such, one of the most common questions I tend to get from new employees is, "How do you keep up with all the new tech, changes, and transformation in the market?" To this, I usually answer, "Optimism." No, optimism is not a business strategy; rather, it's a mindset. Simply, I mean that I am optimistic our team and our company can weather any change by being adaptable and listening to client needs. Skepticism, while fashionable these days, is the enemy of adaptability.

So, you can see why optimism and enthusiasm are great leadership weapons.

When I first started working on the Enterprise Rental Car account almost eight years ago, someone there said to me, "Jared, we don't care how much you know until we know how much you care." That quote still sticks with me.

Show people you care, every hour of every day.

THREE HABIT CHANGES

1. Be sure to make it clear that attitude, enthusiasm, and the how (or the way you approach tasks as opposed to what you do and why) are important to you in a practical way.
2. During your next review cycle, figure out the one thing that your direct report is uniquely great at and help them get even greater. You will get more productivity out of that person if you do that and less of something else.
3. If enthusiasm doesn't come naturally, figure out how to schedule it into your day. This does not make you disingenuous. It makes you good at your job.

YOUR FROM → TO PERSONAL GOAL:

FROM thinking that people will follow you blindly, TO realizing the most optimistic leaders have the most zealous followers.

LESSON 19

NOT EVERY INDIVIDUAL CONTRIBUTOR IS MEANT TO BE A PEOPLE LEADER

"Ever wonder why there are so many VPs and so few leaders?"

—VIPUL KAPADIA, FOUNDER OF THINQSHIFT

Service agencies have the veneer of a management pyramid scheme. Not a real scheme, mind you, rather just the shape of a pyramid in which you get to the top by managing more and more people...even if management is not your superpower.

What you see in the graphic on page 150 is the ladder of individual contribution that usually commences for an entry-level employee at a services firm. In the advertising world, the way this would work would be that every year and a half, on average, Sally would get promoted from intern, to coordinator, to manager, to senior manager, and then on to supervisor. Ninety percent of the reason for promotion has to do with individual skill—how well an employee organizes, how well they think and communicate, how well they optimize search bids, and how well they put copy together. The point is, it's a ladder that is specific to each employee, a "ladder of individual contribution."

So here you have Sally, who is exceeding expectations on her reviews and doing really well and climbing that ladder. Now, there should be a fork in the road that is completely open and entirely based on her core strengths.

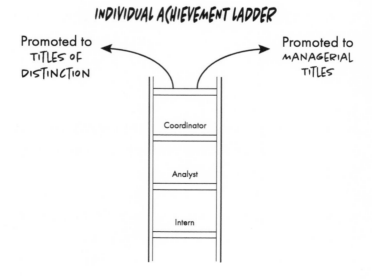

INDIVIDUAL ACHIEVEMENT LADDER

Promoted to
TITLES OF
DISTINCTION

Promoted to
MANAGERIAL
TITLES

Coordinator

Analyst

Intern

There should be a choice and a discussion first about the ideal path of each employee. In truth, some great (and I mean truly great) employees should focus on being the best individual contributor they can be, while others are destined to manage others and scale in a leadership path.

If you end up in the individual contributor category, it's helpful to understand what that might mean for you and what to do about it. Broadly speaking, it means you must continue to keep your specific skills ahead of the market if you want to continue to earn increases in compensation. It means that while others are spending time honing their management skills, you hone your content power.

I have created a simple self-reflection survey below, that your employees (or you) can fill out so you can understand if management is truly your destiny, or perhaps you are a stellar individual contributor.

QUESTIONNAIRE

- On a scale of 1 to 10, how strongly would you rate your desire to manage people when you wake up each morning?
- Which of the two would you prefer doing today: (1) solve a complicated challenge on your computer; or (2) help drive a team toward an end goal?

- What did your last five reviews say was your single best talent?
- When you feel most excited about your job, what are you doing?
- What are the top adjectives used to describe your management style?
- What are you doing when you feel most alive at work?

Respond to these questions honestly, and then discuss with your spouse or partner, and with your manager.

THREE HABIT CHANGES

1. Don't let great individual contributors feel as though they need to become managers. Map out a variety of career paths your team members can travel.
2. Regularly (weekly/monthly/quarterly) analyze and reflect on your career development, asking where your skills are and what you really want.
3. Identify the specific rungs on your personal ladder of individual contribution—which elements of your job are the most important on a daily basis, from interpersonal communication, to optimizing search bids, to organizing status updates—and select one rung to strengthen and improve each week.

YOUR FROM → TO PERSONAL GOAL:

FROM a promotion engine, TO a leader who recognizes and reinforces the value of individual contributors.

MAKE 6S YOUR ENEMY

"My biggest regret is usually hanging on too long."

—RYAN HARRIS, PARTNER, NVP

You're a VP, Client Services Leader, and it's a sunny Thursday and you are walking to work. You're in a good mood. You arrive at your desk and the phone rings.

It's your client and they want to talk.

They no longer think Sally, a member of your team, is delivering the goods. You take it in, you listen, you make notes. Ultimately, you try and work through it mutually.

Another two months go by, and then you hear some new feedback about the quality of work that the team is providing. The reporting and insights are not up to par. The client is frustrated. But you're a cheerleader by nature, right? That's how you got into client leadership, after all. So you buckle down, dedicate more time to coaching, helping, and prodding Sally to greatness. You start to realize, however, that it's not just the client who is feeling this way. You realize that Sally is not feeling that great either. However, Sally is not all that bad, and you have tons of other more pressing problems, you say to yourself, and you move on.

Another month after that, Sally's name comes up on a conference call with the client. It's a slight but a small one. It's a subtle remark, so you barely note it before moving on. Further, you continue to realize Sally is just solid, reliable, and good...just barely good.

Finally, your client calls you up to tell you they are fed up with Sally. They want her off the account, and further, they want a three-month refund for the money on the retainer that she wasted. You somehow feel this is all new information, but in reality, it was laid out for you clearly—you just missed all the telltale signs.

There are two issues. First, there is the matter of lag. Second, you held on to a six.

The first issue is there is a very real lag that you might not be aware of. Here is a picture of that time lag.

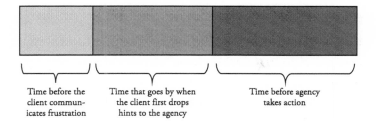

| Time before the client communicates frustration | Time that goes by when the client first drops hints to the agency | Time before agency takes action |

Essentially, there is always lag between the time when you or your client realize someone is not a great employee and the time you take action to exit that person or coach them up with urgency. Lag point one is a killer because, typically, the work suffers for months before anyone has the courage to speak up. Lag point two is the time it takes to decide on a course of action. Lag point three is the time it takes to take the action. In my experience, this overall lag phenomena means that in your head, you might be aware there is a problem and you are taking action, but in reality, far too much time is elapsing that causes more risk to the client relationship and health.

The second issue is that a six can kill a company. In the example of the account manager named Sally, she very clearly could be ranked a six out of ten.

A simple yet classic rating system for performance at a services firm is a scale of one through ten, where ten is the highest. Some of the best commentary about this comes from a *New York Times* article on the tyranny of the six.* In the spirit of oversimplification, it suggests that 1s, 2s, 3s, and 4s are folks who are a poor fit for the organization. It does not mean they are not great people or employees, just that they don't fit in on your team. At the other end are the 8s, 9s, and 10s, who are fantastic in general, or specifically having a great year. This leaves us with the 5s, 6s, and 7s.

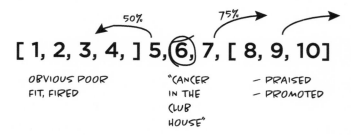

The 5s, well—in theory, they would have a chance at salvation and could find their way to becoming a 7, 8, 9, or 10, but they look up and set their bar too low based on what they see from the 6. Accordingly, they have an even greater chance than need be at falling into the 1–4 pile and finding the exit. The 7, ordinarily, would have a 75 percent chance to move into the 8–10 zone and celebrate amongst the best employees; only, they look down, see that the 6 is still in the office and determine that 6 is the bar. Now the 7 has a greater chance than need be of ending up in the wrong pile.

---

* Jay Goltz, "The Dirty Little Secret of Successful Companies," *New York Times*, February 8, 2011, https://boss.blogs.nytimes.com/2011/02/08/the-dirty-little-secret-of-successful-companies/?_r=1.

So what of the 6? Well, you see the erosion the 6 causes. No, they are not your biggest problem in that they are not a raging fire you must deal with. But as you can see, like a cancer, they eat your organization from the inside.

Yes, the 6 could be meeting expectations occasionally. But as the client leader, it's your job to help them not just meet expectations but to exceed them and join the 7+ group or show them the door.

Meanwhile, you are also in charge of the whole health of the team and client and business (*sigh*, you have a hard job), which means you must be the person to also raise the flag when you see the person stalled out and regressing in to 5-ville. If it were easy, anyone could do it. But it's not easy. The key is to find the right leaders who don't put up with 6s.

A favorite quote I recently heard was, "A's hire other A's, and B's hire C's."

Find 10s who want to hire other 10s, who collectively have zero tolerance for 6s.

Understanding what harm a 6 can do, let's spend some time talking about strategies for how to identify, coach, and exit.

Strategy 1: Ensure your firm's review system creates some level of confrontation. If you have a ten-point system, for example, it creates too many places to hide (five, six, seven). Less complex systems create more clarity and more choice. I have seen a simple one-to-five scale as the best. One's and two's are compassionately exited, four's and five's are exceeding, where a three is just meeting expectations. That is clear. There are too many systems that create so many available grades that it allows managers to avoid having difficult conversations.

Strategy 2: Don't distribute spoils equally. The best people should be getting disproportionate awards in the form of bonuses, compensation, coaching, and assignments. It becomes very easy during merit-and-review season to start from a point of worrying about person X leaving if they don't get a certain percentage raise. Instead, start with the core people who are moving the needle and ensure they really know they matter.

Above all else, be ruthless in figuring out where the 6s are hiding and make it clear to your company that you do not tolerate it.

Strategy 3: Exit people with compassion and decisiveness. I encourage leaders to come to the right decision as to whether someone is a six first, and then figure out the exit plan. Too often, leaders conflate those two decisions, causing delay. Once you know that someone is not right for the organization, you can quickly spend more time on the most humane thing you can do, which is a compassionate exit plan. When leaders dither and invent PIP (performance improvement plans) and other instruments, even though they know the person is not right, it creates mutual stress. Remember, if you know that person is not doing a great job, they likely know it as well and don't feel great about coming to work either.

THREE HABIT CHANGES

1. My core advice is to ensure your firm's review system creates some level of confrontation to weed out your 6s. A scale that I have seen work is a simple one-to-five scale. This creates a true decision-making moment and forces a critical conversation to be had with the employee if they are a three.
2. Focus each quarter on your three's and how to get them up the ladder, or compassionately to another, more fitting role. Focus even more on your five's.
3. Be more rigorous around watching for time lag. You won't ever feel you moved too quickly, but you might feel you moved too slowly.

YOUR FROM → TO PERSONAL GOAL:

FROM a leader who tolerates good employees, TO a leader

who moves faster on talent decisions and sets the bar for others.

LESSON 21

FOCUS

"I feel laser-focused on the important right now."

—ERIC SPETT, CEO OF TERMINUS

In order to get the most out of your team, you need to be clear and focused about what is important and what actually moves the needle. As a leader, you will be defined more by what you say no to than by what you say yes to. The opening quote comes from Eric Spett, who is CEO of Terminus, one of the fastest growing B2B software companies in the United States. As CEO of a high-growth company, there are hundreds of things Eric could do every day. However, what Eric does so well is to ask himself not what could be accomplished today, but rather what should be accomplished with focus to move the needle. Eric, more so than most young leaders I have gotten to know over the years, is tremendous at separating the important from the urgent and ensuring that he makes it clear to his leadership team what is important to him. For Eric, this did not come naturally—nor is it natural for anyone really. Focus takes work. Clarity takes work. Saying no to distraction takes work. Feeling comfortable with being unpopular yet respected takes time and work. I would encourage those reading this book to use a few of the strategies in this lesson to help you on your journey to become a principled leader who makes focus a hallmark of your leadership style.

There are two very simple devices you can use for this.

First, create a NINETY-day planning document.

I've created a table (see next page) that combines features I have seen from great partners and friends over the years. First, I like how the goals link to objectives, to keys to success, and to deliverables. It's linear and easy to follow, so anyone on your team can pick it up and find it useful.

The second part of this grid is the "Now, Next, New" concept, which allows you to contextualize the goals from a timeline perspective. "Now" should be what needs to get done in the next thirty to ninety days, while "Next" is thinking about the overall vision of the leadership. "New" should be what gets thought about for next year, or beyond the one-year time period. At the very least, going through the exercise of completing one of these grids is critical for success. A person in client services will simply bounce from client directive to client directive. The Great Client Partner will chart a course to mutual greatness, and that makes all the difference.

CEO GOAL	OBJECTIVES/ GOALS	KEYS TO SUCCESS	DELIVERABLES	TIMELINE/ DEPENDENCIES
1	Now			
	New			
	Next			
2	Now			
	New			
	Next			
3	Now			
	New			
	Next			

Use this grid for your ninety-day planning strategy and continue to update it as a living, breathing document with your team.

Second, Franklin Covey's Urgent vs. Nonurgent Prioritization Grid

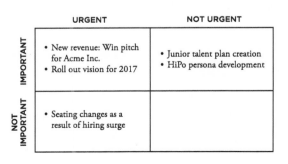

	URGENT	NOT URGENT
IMPORTANT	• New revenue: Win pitch for Acme Inc. • Roll out vision for 2017	• Junior talent plan creation • HiPo persona development
NOT IMPORTANT	• Seating changes as a result of hiring surge	

This is one of the most famous, effective, and simple organizational constructs to prioritization. The key to using this grid is to be practical and tough minded on how you categorize items. The common urge is to put everything in the upper-left box, but that is simply not possible. Something that is both urgent and important means it's timely (must happen in the next quarter) and will also move the needle on the business you represent. Things that go in the upper-left box should be items that are both very timely in nature and also will move the company forward. The common theme for the upper-left box must be items of consequence. Examples of things that would go into the "Urgent/Important" quadrant could be upcoming business reviews, new business pitches, client crises, or staffing shortages.

If simple management frameworks don't inspire you to think about the importance of focus, then I would suggest looking to politics for additional inspiration.

In 2012, Barack Obama earned 70 percent of the vote in Cuyahoga County. This was a county in the all-important battleground state of Ohio. It is the densely populated urban area that contains Cleveland. Arguably, that won him the election even though Romney was winning in the suburban (and less populated) counties surrounding Cleveland.* Obama realized this was a county where, with

---

* Frank Bruni, "The Millions of Marginalized Americans," *New York Times*, July 25, 2015, https://www.nytimes.com/2015/07/26/opinion/sunday/frank-bruni-the-millions-of-marginalized-americans.html?_r=0.

reasonable effort, he could take a massive chunk of the vote. So he focused time, energy, money, advertising, and political operatives on this county. Essentially, the lesson in Cuyahoga County is to focus on what moves the needle, and where you can win an unfair fight.

The idea of Cuyahoga County is that you can't be amazing at everything, everywhere, every time. With focus and a close look at the odds of success, you can find wins. It is also a very telling story of how research up front and a lens of maximum output for the least possible input is the right currency in client leadership.

Whether the ninety-day plan inspires you or perhaps the urgent/important prioritization grid, or even the Cuyahoga County story, all that matters is that you look yourself and your team in the eyes and demand greater focus. Demand of yourself relentless pursuit of the important, and don't let the urgent run your business.

THREE HABIT CHANGES

1. Use the Urgent/Important grid at the start of every quarter. Have those who report to you do the same to ensure your visions are aligned.
2. Utilize a ninety-day planning sheet to ensure you have a plausible and detailed plan of attack. Also, distribute this to those who report directly to you.

3. Be flexible on your planning tools. They can and should change with time. The important thing is that you're clear about your goals and how they impact your team members (and how your team members are essential in helping you achieve those goals).

YOUR FROM → TO PERSONAL GOAL:

FROM a leader who bounces from one thing to another, TO a principled leader who applies a laser focus to needle moving and important opportunities.

PART 3

BEHAVE LIKE
A LEADER

DON'T CONFUSE LIKE AND LOVE, AND AVOID SWEATPANTS!

"Who does this client love? Who is the one person this client absolutely cannot live without?"

—SARAH HOFSTETTER, FORMER CEO
OF 360i, PRESIDENT COMSCORE

If you don't know whether your client loves at least a few people on your team, then you are closer to getting fired than you are to getting a renewal.

I would advise you to keep yourself honest by keeping an inventory of client satisfaction as it relates to your team members. This is not just another net-promoter type survey. Instead, this is a love survey. It is very important to be honest with yourself. The idea is pictured in the next chart. To put it simply, as the leader, you keep a running tally of each of your team members and how you see them perceived by the client. If you see too many "likes" and not enough "loves" on your chart, then pause and ask yourself and your team how to raise the bar to love. Remember, the idea here is not to be fake or to try and force love. Love comes with time, trust, respect, wins, fights, and being in the trenches together.

CLIENT	Q1	Q2	Q3	Q4
Billy	Love	Love	Love	Love
Sally	Love	Like	Like	Love
Jason	Like	Like	Hate	Like

Why care so much about love and why pick that word in the first place? Love triggers a different stimulation in the brain than simply liking a person. It's more intense. You want your clients to feel something profound when they think of your team: genuine fondness and total trust. Like, on the other hand, is a practical consideration. You can share a cubicle with someone you like, but your relationship with someone you love can weather much more than that.

You don't fire love. You fire like. Love is harder to earn, but it lasts longer.

Beyond just taking the pulse of how clients feel about your individual team members, it's important to help your team get in a position to be loved in the first place. Here is a good example of a worksheet you can create for you and your team to try and jumpstart some love if it's not there naturally.

LOVE INVENTORY

WHAT CLIENTS MIGHT BE LOOKING FOR IN THEIR AGENCY (THEY LOVE)?	LIST ACHIEVEMENTS IN THE PAST THREE MONTHS
Exposes me to thinking about something in a different way than I had previously	
Brings skillsets we do not have in-house	
Makes me look smart	
Helps me understand and contextualize what my competition is doing in this space	
Brings me actionable insights	
Gives me a regular holistic look at the health of what we're doing for them	
Understands my brand	
Synthesizes data, gleans meaningful insights, and evolves measurement	
Collaborates with internal and external partners	
Provides strategic thought leadership	
Vertical knowledge	
Brings me new suggestions of things to do to help my business	
Exposes me to new platforms with analysis of why it's good or not good for my business	

So, how do you cultivate love from your clients while still being authentic and real?

FIVE GOLDEN RULES

Respond ridiculously fast and show bias toward names, dates, and Key Performance Indicators (KPIs)—If this needs explaining, put down this book, back away slowly, and find a new gig. Fair or unfair, a client won't love you if they don't think you care. Sarah Hofstetter is a longtime friend and a founder of so many firsts in the advertising industry. One of her simple mantras is instructive to the Great Client Partner: "If it does not have a name, a date, and a KPI...it is not real." She's right. If you send a rally email, and you have not assigned owners, dates for deliverables, and how each will be measured, you are not leading.

Don't say yes all the time. A well-considered no can go a long way—I remember a talented VP Group Account Director who gained more eventual business by telling the client to take their performance creative business to a partner who specialized in cheap production and lightning speed. This allowed the client to create more banners, segmented in more granular ways, which in turn helped the client and even us as their agency. This exceptional VP understood this was a time where a "no...and" was a lot more useful than a yes. Trust was built on the memory sticker that we did not give all recommendations based on our own bottom line. On the other side of the coin, I worked with a very senior person who always answered, "Yes, no problem" whenever he was asked a hard-nosed question by a client. That just eroded credibility.

Have thoughts that lead—Today it's not good enough to be a character from *Mad Men*. No concert or bottle of wine can make up for the frustration a client will feel about you if you clog up the works as opposed to add value. Beyond just helping the system move fast, challenge yourself to have thoughts that lead. Don't just rely on the SMEs, or you will make yourself obsolete. Invest in this through reading, curiosity, and listening more than talking. What it means to have thoughts that lead sounds simple, but it's not easy. It means you have to do your own exploration and then know how to synthesize that into predictions and implications.

Make sure you're not wearing sweatpants—When you are in a relationship for many years with someone, you might show up in sweatpants for a casual evening. This is something you would never have done when trying to win their heart all those years ago, however. You would have brought flowers, done your hair, and put on your best clothes to impress. Perhaps if you have a patient spouse, you can get away with sweatpants in marriage. But you certainly can't do so in a client-based business. Do what you need to do as a Great Client Partner to do a sweatpants inventory. Ask your team a few basic questions:

- What is the last new thing we have done for the client?
- Are we making weekly calls exciting, or are we just rolling over the playbook?
- What is the last innovative idea we have brought this client?
- When did we last shake up the team?

Avoid sweatpants at all costs.

Always communicate in plain English—Clients hate doublespeak and jargon. People use bigger words when trying to confuse a client or when they don't understand the facts. Try and use fewer words and words that are simple. Don't say, "We will touch base once we get traction," when you can more easily say, "We have work to do, and we will get back to you by August 12 with answers."

THREE HABIT CHANGES

1. Do a quarterly inventory of what—and who—your client is responding to on your team, both positively and negatively.
2. Think of ways you can help your client beyond what's in the SOW. How can you make your contact's life easier? Can you even get him or her promoted?

3. Listen to yourself when you speak and read your writing. Are you using unnecessary jargon? Regularly make a list of unnecessarily complex words you might be using too frequently and practice simplifying your communication.

FROM liked TO loved.

LESSON 23

GET UP AND DRAW

Leaders must persuade for a living. At times, they also have to be peacekeepers or arbiters. The most basic problem with human relationships has to do with fighting over words. When you fight over words, the fight tends to continue on and on because people develop an attachment to their own words, manner of speech, and their belief system. From that vantage point, it becomes harder to find compromise and progress. Let's look at a real verbal exchange between an account person and a client I witnessed:

Client: I need that production estimate within the next ten hours.

Account Manager: I can't do that. It's too fast a turnaround request.

Client: Do you mean to tell me you can't be nimble?

AM: We are very nimble. We just don't have enough people on the team to handle that timeline.

Client: Are you now telling me you need to add FTEs and money all because I need a simple production quote? Agency Y would be much faster. I just want something done fast, and now you are telling me we have a staffing issue.

AM: No, that is not what I meant to say. Um...I just need to push back here a bit and ask that we prioritize this request given the other items you have asked for.

Client: Frankly, I think I already get enough push-back.

And it goes on and on. Words just seem to spin and create ill will sometimes. Here, we witness an account person trying to advocate for quality work, timelines, and even prioritization. We see a client advocating for a nimble world. In truth, they want the same thing, but they can't hear each other.

All they can hear are these keywords that are sparking off their worst instincts.

The war of words allows for almost no middle ground

or genuine problem-solving. As account managers, the holy grail is to create the space in which two parties can illustrate what they need and paint a way forward.

I submit that the key is to get up and draw.

In the entire human catalog of arguments, every issue can be arbitrated with five basic drawings, which I've created here. If mastered, these illustrations allow great leaders to achieve nirvana in arbitration and problem-solving in most tense situations.

SITUATION 1: THE MOUNTAIN TO CLIMB

You have a client that has one hundred thousand unique users and insists on reaching a million. This seems like a grueling mountain to climb, and even the client is skeptical of the ability to improve ten times over. How do you make them confident in your plan versus one that perhaps seems like it was hatched on the spot? The key is to reverse engineer your thesis, unpack it, and make it seem as substantive as it actually is. The other key is to get the client to get into the mix with you and debate the different sources of growth. Debate is good. Silence is danger.

So get up and draw.

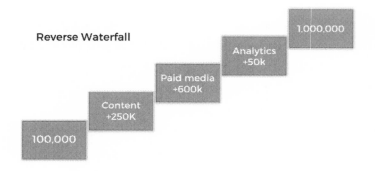

Reverse Waterfall

The reverse waterfall is a famous construct taken mostly from the consulting field and was taught to me by Jason Trevison, CFO at CarGurus and a board member of LegalZoom. It does two things exceptionally well. It takes what could seem like an insurmountable goal and breaks it down into achievable composite parts.

Second, it gets you and the client talking, almost horse trading, between what components are likely to ladder up to the larger goal. The point here, as in all these drawings, is that you and the client are now talking, and even more important, the client now sees a believable plan of attack that is both numerical and descriptive.

SITUATION 2: TOO MANY IDEAS

Picture yourself in a swirling brainstorm with multiple agencies, consultants, tech providers, and clients. Ideas are flying around like gnats. There seems to be no rudder. The problem is not too many ideas, but rather there are too many good ideas. Or perhaps too many good ideas from too many people, with too many motives. What do you do?

What is needed here is the four-box filter. It is as basic as possible, so simple my kids could draw it. And that is the genius behind this drawing. It creates choice. Choice is difficult. What was harder in college, writing a tight, cohesive three-page paper, or vomiting up twenty pages containing anything you could think of? Being selective is hard. However, guiding smart choices is the very core of a Great Client Partner.

Simple 4-box filter

	SAFE SINGLE	HOME RUN SWING
NOW		
NEXT		

I also like this framework because it has two dimensions: time and impact. The top axis is about the size of the idea, while the vertical axis addresses when this can be accomplished. Experiment with this construct, but there are plenty of other ways to label the grid, which is why it's so powerful. Steve Jobs famously used it when he made his comeback to Apple to help his team of engineers simplify the number of products they were making.

SITUATION 3: TOO MANY FEATURES

You are working with your client on delivering a brand new website. They have a large wish list of features they want to include. As the client leader in the room, you feel worried, and the client feels like the agency or consulting firm is saying no a lot. How do you make this meeting more productive?

You use a prioritization chart.

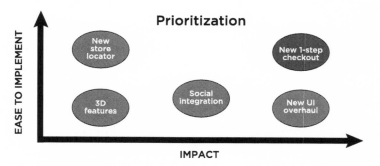

This illustration works really well on the fly. The best thing about it is that you can make it interactive and give your client the marker, or put these up with Velcro and let the client come up and share their view about where things should be plotted.

SITUATION 4: MISUSED RESOURCES

You are the media lead on a piece of digital business. Your team seems to be spending a lot of time on reporting that does not appear to be valued by the client, and it's certainly not important to your team. Soon, you find this person is spending so much time on reporting that they are not optimizing the media. The client needs reporting, but you need this person working on the media. Meanwhile, procurement is hardly interested in your plight.

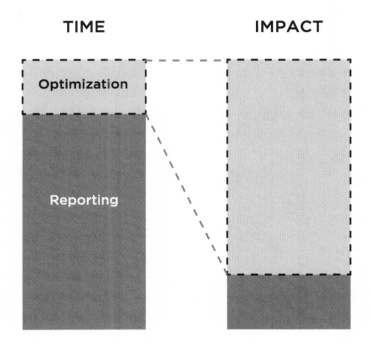

This is a 100 percent stacked bar that matches input (resources) against output (desired outcome). It's meant to show that what you are doing is either aligned with the desired outcome of a project or it's not. What this graph illustrates in our example is that 80 percent of the time of the team is being spent on reporting, yet they are only delivering 20 percent of the output and value.

This graph is meant to be a blunt instrument, but play it out. At least now the client can grab the marker, hit the whiteboard and counter with a different percentage. At least you are both now debating the drawing and not each other's language. Essentially, the drawing has become the mediator.

STAR GRID

The STAR Grid is another way to tackle this scenario. It uses the Situation-Threat-Action-Result format. It allows you to write something on a whiteboard and then debate with the client about how to size up the situation. It provides for only a small amount of space, which forces both you and the client to be concise in your remarks and how you size up the situation and conflict.

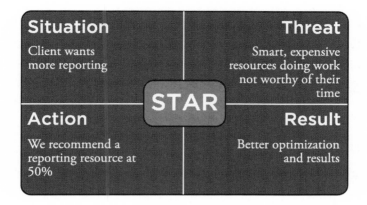

Situation
Client wants more reporting

Threat
Smart, expensive resources doing work not worthy of their time

STAR

Action
We recommend a reporting resource at 50%

Result
Better optimization and results

THREE HABIT CHANGES

1. Next time you feel conflict between your team or with your client, use one of these drawings. Get up and draw!
2. Teach the drawings and the concepts behind them to the junior people on your team, and give them opportunities to put them into practice.
3. Get your client used to the notion that all meetings will have whiteboard moments.

YOUR FROM → TO PERSONAL GOAL:

FROM someone who allows escalation of words and rhetoric, TO leading successful mediations and productive debate via drawing and framing.

LESSON 24

COMMUNICATE WITHOUT BS

"I don't use fancy words and am not as smooth as others I compete against, but people understand what I say, and I am consistent with my words and deeds."

—BRUCE BELSKY, ATTORNEY AND DAD

The problem for the current eighteen-to-twenty-nine-year-old generation is that they are facing three headwinds:

- There is a culture of buzzwords that is here to stay.
- There is massive discomfort with conflict.
- The art of brevity is gone.

This has led to identifying three deadly communication sins in the workplace:

- Burying the lede and weaselly openings—these are weak, muddled opening statements.
- Using a passive voice—when you say, "Mistakes were made," as opposed to, "I made a mistake," you conceal who's responsible.
- Ending weakly—this happens when you don't have specific actions to take.

Fear not. There are a few things you can do to improve how you communicate (if it's your problem) or improve how you coach plainspokenness (if you are in the mentor role).

HEADLINES

The key phrase here to understand is "don't bury the lede." It's important to understand the power of starting your email or presentation with the main fact you want to convey. Look at these before-and-after examples of a simulated email I'm drafting to my boss. These are meant to show the power of the headline.

BEFORE:

Sarah, hope all is well. We both know that, for years, we have wanted to invest further into our performance creative capability. I think the marriage of creative and data continues on full force. With dynamic creative that can be fueled by CRM data, this field gets so interesting and of further importance to our clients. We should really explore this and gather the leadership to figure out next steps.

AFTER:

Sarah, using CRM data for better creative solutions is critical, and we should have an A+ solution in market by Q4. I will arrange a meeting for the key people by the end of this week, prepare a preread and agenda, and lead this project. Do I have your permission to continue?

Nothing frustrates senior executives more than circuitous writing or fluff. Lead with the headline, follow with an action item, and then close with a deadline to act. Trust me on this. I know from experience. My chairman once went out and bought an hourglass to help reinforce brevity on my part. I only wish I was joking. Granted, I am certain I was not the only reason, but I sure can tell you I was part of it.

He would tend to ask me smart and open questions, such as, "Jared, how is the team doing?" Traditionally, my answer would start with color commentary on each and every team member, and then, after several minutes, I would get to the headline: "Morale is very strong right now, our best team in years." That was all he needed to hear.

Just about any executive worth their salt wants to hear every answer in the following format:

Headline first (one sentence)

+ one supporting detail

+ one concern

+ what you are doing to address that concern

Use this recipe for headlines and keep your boss from buying an hourglass.

ACTIVE VOICE

Using an active voice is a key trait to persuasion for an account person.

Look at the mundane matters in the example below and notice how important using the active voice is, even in those sentences. In active voice, the subject is doing the acting, and with the passive voice, the subject is being acted upon. Passive voice often results in sentences that are longer than necessary or that needlessly obscure the subject that the verb relates to.

ACTIVE	PASSIVE
	↓
→	
Subject is doing the acting	Subject is being acted upon, receiving the action.

ACTIVE	PASSIVE
Billy is building a house.	A house is being built by Billy.
You stole the cookie from the jar.	The cookie was stolen from the jar by you.
I can't get no satisfaction.	No satisfaction can be gotten by me.
Neil said yes.	Things were said.

Like everyone, clients relish straightforward conversation and speech patterns. Don't say, "An error has been made, and we are very sorry," when you can and should say, "Our team made an error. The cost implication is $12,000. We will format a plan to rebate that money by January 12. Thank you for your patience, and we are sorry."

Here is a great example of a jumbled BS email, what the client likely took from it, and then the better version of what should have been authored.

What was written:

"Team members are working twelve-hour days to accommo-

date our daily workload, which I've come to discern as not the exception but the norm. I would like to partner with you on the solve. This is not just for July, but moving forward in hopes to find a better place where the right work is getting done by the right people with the right priority. Please let me know if you're open for a discussion on how to solve."

What the client heard:

I can't manage my world right now and need help doing my job. My feelings are also getting involved, so really, I'd just like a hug and some ice cream, and maybe you to tell me what to do next.

A better more active version:

There is a conflict of priority with the current number of deliverables under deadline. Based on our attention to recent conversations, we propose to act upon the following prioritization schedule unless you suggest otherwise.

Deliverable X—Friday
Deliverable Y—the following week
Deliverable Z—the first week of October

Let us know if there are any concerns with this approach and we will discuss a new solution. Thanks!

PLAIN ENGLISH

Speaking in plain English just means using simple words, as opposed to buzzwords, overly technical, specialized jargon, and speaking as a human. Over the years, it seems truth and grit have been polished away in favor of obfuscation. When is the last time you had someone at work tell you that he "just plain dropped the ball?" It probably doesn't happen too often. Instead, people have a tendency to complicate their responses in order to save face, but this usually backfires. Even though most people learned as children that when you try to hide the fact that you made a mistake by being clever with language, you were still going to be found out, usually through a series of uncomfortable interrogations of your speech. So just be up front at the beginning.

Also, people use twenty words when a few will do. What I can tell you is that executives are desperately searching for people who will share bad news as fast as they will share good news. On the client side, they are desperate for agency partners who speak in simple terms and can be trusted.

POWERFUL ENDINGS

This is the art and craft of always ending an email with some action statement.

Too many emails trail off: "And so we will circle back and regroup and all get together within the next month or so to talk about progress." Not that I don't like to circle back as much as the next American, but this is a call for nothing.

I have a good friend named Anthony. Anthony has had a great career as the head of sales for one of the best tech companies in the country. Besides being a relatively good-looking and tall Italian guy, charismatic, and a scratch golfer who can also sing, he happens to be loved by clients because he is not just passionate about their world, but they can always understand him. If his team is not performing well, he is the first to put his arm around the client and say, "Listen, Bob, I need to be the first one to tell you that we are bleeping the bed and not living up to the promises we made you. I am going to get our top three minds in a room and get you a plan of attack within forty-eight hours that will get us back to where we should be. I am sorry. This is important to me."

Anthony understands the power of plain English combined with passion.

THREE HABIT CHANGES

1. Make a game of it to keep jargon in-check. When someone on your team talks about "gaining traction," for example, call them out politely. Words that should

be pointed out might include (but aren't limited to): circle back, marinate, stakeholders, strategic, missed the mark. The point here is that if you, as a leader, do not correct useless language, you are condoning it.

2. Go find fifty random emails you have written to clients recently. Print them out and highlight every sentence where you know you sound like a bag of hot air. Circle buzzwords as well as every sentence where you say nothing but take thirty words to do so. Now, go ahead and see how much yellow you have. Is that how you want to sound?

3. Before sending an email, read it again, start to finish, and ask yourself if it has a ring of authenticity to it. If not, rewrite it in a way you wish people would communicate with you.

YOUR FROM → TO PERSONAL GOAL:

FROM indirect and passive language patterns, TO a direct and active voice.

LESSON 25

AVOID COMMUNICATION SINS

Client leaders are always on the frontline. Most of your actions are responses to hairy issues. Given that, you can count on the fact that you often need to communicate under some level of pressure. Not falling into pressure-related communication traps like the ones described in the previous lesson is an essential attribute of the Great Client Partner. Here are some more strategies to improve your communication.

PRO TIP: USE YOUR EMAIL DRAFTS

For processing your thoughts, prioritizing your messages, and just getting out your frustrations, email drafts are cheaper than a therapist and just as effective. Your employees, clients, and partners (and maybe even loved ones) will thank you for venting your thoughts in a draft that you'll never actually send.

This is a visual from the actual panel on the left side of my inbox (at time of picture). It shows I had drafted almost four thousand emails that never went out. I began those emails but then never sent them, all for various reasons.

The top two reasons are:

1. To count to ten
2. To better finish the thought with more rigor

Of the two, counting to ten is the real reason I use my email drafts. The truth is it takes no courage or management ability to hammer out a mean, rude, or angry email. For a brief moment, it feels better than anything to get your frustrations out on a keyboard and write "WTF" or some such oblique phrase, but it takes greater discipline to hold that email. So what I might do is draft it and then count to ten, maybe sleep on it for a night, and then do a ton of deleting and corrections the next day. You will be a far better leader if you get into that habit.

What's more, it's a sad truth that email can make or break your career as a client leader. Tone, timing, and content all have to be perfect, and that is difficult if you are a living, breathing, emotional person, and not a cyborg.

Before sending, you might even want to print out the email, read it out loud and ask yourself a simple question. Could you comfortably say this out loud if someone you respected was in the room with you?

BE OLD SCHOOL

I mean it. Be Miles Davis. Be old school. Be jazz.

We have enough corporate pop stars who run huge machines focused only on bringing attention to themselves. In a lot of ways, that's great, but being old school in a new school world only makes being old school cooler.

There are some ways to communicate that are always in style and always certain to gratify your listeners. For instance, write handwritten notes to your clients. Don't do it just to say "Thank you" from time to time, but do it randomly, spontaneously.

Walk the halls and talk to the people you work with. Be friendly and commit random acts of kindness by surprising your coworkers or clients with a small gift, even doughnuts.

And show gratitude every time someone does something like that for you.

AVOID THE SEVEN DEADLY VERBAL SINS OF CLIENT LEADERSHIP

Related to communicating extremely well over email, there are some things to learn about how to communicate verbally. Here's a list of seven things not to say, for various reasons.

- **"Yes, we can do that."** A client asks you if it is possible to turn around a new forecast in six hours. Without thinking, the client leader says, "Yes, we can do that." This is a double sin. It sells out your team without them having a chance to weigh in, and it also shows your client that you are a yes-person.
- **"We will get the A team on it."** If you need to say you will put the A team on it, it implies the B team might have been on it previously. Why do you even have a B team? Never rank things out loud in that fashion.
- **"Yeah, I thought that work was poor as well."** Why would you ever admit that? It purely suggests you're a wimp who would sell anyone out for a nickel. If you thought it was bad (which is fine), then you should

have spoken up to delay the meeting, asking for more time till you had something worthwhile to present.

- **"We will circle back on that one."** Great, now you angered them and made the client feel like you don't want to address the problem. Never delay anything you can finish up at that moment. Don't ever give a client the Heisman stiff-arm. Face the music the minute you can. Don't circle back.
- **"We'll have a slide for that later."** Bravo, you guessed right and made a slide in preparation. Now, stop making this all about showing off your prep work and just be a bit more improvisational. Get to the issue the client wants to speak about when they want to speak about it. Why put them off just because the slide sequence says so?
- **"That department is harder to get in touch with."** No client cares about how your agency or consultancy sausage is made. Enough said.
- **"We will redouble our efforts."** Clients pay for achievement, not activity. They pay for results, not effort. The client is not your mom, who used to give you an ice pop and a gold star because you tried hard during elementary school. This is the big leagues. Don't tell a client you will redouble your efforts. Instead, tell them what specifically you will do differently and who will help you achieve that.

Throughout every interaction, ensure that you're communicating in a way that reminds your clients and your team members how reliable you are.

THREE HABIT CHANGES

1. Don't put the recipient's address in your emails until the moment you're ready to hit send. That way you won't accidentally send something written in the heat of the moment. Write several drafts of each important message.
2. Be old school. Write a handwritten note to someone.
3. Practice not saying any of the Seven Deadly Verbal Sins. Review that list until you know it intimately. Pay attention to the spirit of those statements so you always put the client first, letting them know they're in good hands.

YOUR FROM → TO PERSONAL GOAL:

FROM a leader that shoots, readies, and aims, TO a leader who avoids pitfalls through patience.

LESSON 26

BE PATIENT IN YOUR CAREER

"Would you make a career decision for a raise equal to the price of a Starbucks coffee?"

—SOMETHING I OFTEN ASK OTHERS

Do the math. In your twenties, it was very common to see someone move jobs for $5,000 more somewhere else. But let's deconstruct that for a minute. After taxes, $5,000 leaves you with $3,250. Let's divide that by 365 days and we end up with less than $9 a day. While that is nothing to sneeze at—all money is relevant and helpful—it is certainly about the cost of a coffee and a scone at Starbucks. I would argue that is not reason enough to leave a good position.

There is not a ton of patience in the services workforce. Average tenures range from eighteen to twenty-four months. This has gotten worse now that ad-tech—and the likes of Facebook and Google—are on the hunt for talent. Promotions are expected in yearly increments. Expectation management is at an all-time low, which compounds the problem. Young managers must do a better job helping those who work for them understand that Rome was not built in a day, and they would be better off for having helped their reports understand that it takes time to build skills and graduate to new titles.

Okay, so how do you, as an aspiring leader, help change the narrative at your company or on your team?

Helping people understand divergent ways of thinking, as well as setting better expectations, can help dramatically. Specifically, I would suggest having crucial conversations three months before review season, not during it, to get a better understanding of what your employee is assuming in terms of promotions and timing.

People expect a constant ascent. We are used to the ladder metaphor, step up after step up, higher and higher. In truth, what happens—or should happen—is that after you reach a new rung, the bar is raised, and accordingly, your performance actually dips, relative to that new bar. That is not a bad thing—it's normal. What is bad is that most managers don't explain this, and often the first review after a promotion is a tough one. Billy thinks he's crushing it when his manager thinks he has not yet lived up to the promotion.

TWO MINDSETS—NOT EQUALLY SMART

There tend to be two mindsets, Patient Patricia and Job Jumping Jimmy.

Jimmy is a typical services employee. He jumps from job to job every two years or so. For every jump, he secures between $5,000 to $10,000 more in salary and benefits. Each jump appears to be a win for Jimmy. He is earning more money and accruing more titles faster than his peer, Patient Patricia. But that is only on the surface. What is also happening is that Jimmy's titles and earnings are outpacing his output and performance, and there is a spotlight on him from management.

Meanwhile, there's Patient Patricia. Patricia, as the next graph shows, stays at each job for at least four years. At each employer, Patricia creates connections. She finds a boss who cares about her beyond a transactional nature. That boss gives her the critical feedback she needs (and deserves) to do a better job. Patient Patricia has developed a relationship with a mentor who will advocate for her. When that mentor leaves to go to another company, that mentor will suggest Patricia for jobs she never even knew existed. She gets meaningful but inexpensive experience and nurtured moments to test out new managerial traits. She is supported. Patricia has created a path to being an adaptable leader with no ceiling to her career.

Kudos Patricia.

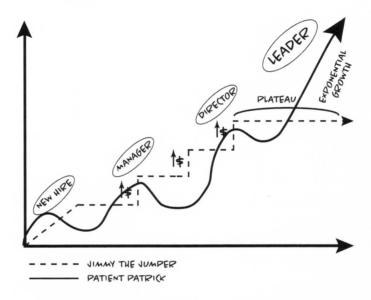

There are five things that allow Patricia to thrive long term while Jimmy fizzles out over his short-term decisions that amount, after taxes, to be a Starbucks coffee, a fancy scone, and maybe, some of those waffle cookies they sell.

Patricia does the following: she LEARNs.

Learn—Make it a point to learn one new hard skill every year. Learn to sew. Learn to make pottery. Learn to code.

Learn statistics. Stay in a learning mindset. The more time you spend in one position, the cheaper at-bats you're going to get; that is, more learning opportunities will open up for you.

Execute—Stay in one job long enough to excel, getting into a better situation and position for truly beneficial advancement.

Adapt—Understand that at each new promotion, there is also a step backward, demanding new skills, and EQ (emotional intelligence) to reflect on what must be done better and differently.

Rabbi (Mentor)—Find someone who can tell you the whole truth, stick up for you, and give you the inside scoop. You are nothing without an advocate.

Network—Be a family person, be balanced, but don't forget to network, too—especially when you don't immediately need anything. A desperate networker is someone who is transparently using other people for their own gain.

The problem with job jumping is that you're a winner—until you are a big time loser. Jimmy never has the chance to LEARN. He is a transactional figment of others' imaginations who ends up with too high a salary at the age of thirty-one but who has not acquired the skills to keep it going. Job jumping makes Jimmy flop by age thirty-two.

Be Patient Patricia, not Jumping Jimmy.

THREE HABIT CHANGES

1. Stay for four. If you stay for much less than four years at a job, especially in the services industry, assume you did not make enough of a human connection for someone to advocate for you in rooms you are not in. Stay for four. Stay for four. Stay for four.
2. Don't eat alone. Ask someone senior for breakfast or lunch once a week. Nobody says no to a good meal and a chance to impart some wisdom. Go ahead and try it—it will change your career. It did mine.
3. Get cheap at-bats. Volunteer to do things, on others' dimes, where you might fail but where the price of failure is small. For example, if you are not naturally very analytical, volunteer to help author the weekly report, or help compile the financials so you practice that side of your brain in a safe environment. Think of them as batting practice. You can swing for the fences, and if you miss, you don't actually strike out.

YOUR FROM → TO PERSONAL GOAL:

FROM finding jobs, TO active career management.

LESSON 27

BE THE REASON YOUR TEAM LOVES TO COME TO WORK, NOT WHY THEY QUIT

"People accidentally lie during their exit interview."

—ERIC BACAOLOS, FORMER CTO OF 360i, CONDUCTOR, AND W20 GROUP

The majority of folks who quit tend to cite salary and title in their exit interview. This is a lie. People lie not because they're bad or want to hide the truth, but rather because the truth is complicated, hurtful, and hard to put a finger on.

But here are some more insights from HR professionals I trust and respect. They have helped me see the three fundamental reasons people actually quit a service organization:

- People quit if they think their direct boss is an idiot.
- People quit if they don't understand the mission and vision of the company and, further, if they don't understand how their contributions fit in with that vision.
- People quit if they can't get their best work done because of artificial barriers like politics, too many meetings, or requiring silly permissions.

Okay, that indicates it is the CEO's job to ensure folks don't quit, right?

Wrong.

Another of my favorite phrases that I tend to use is that everything to do with HR is a team sport. HR can't solve every retention issue. Neither can the CEO. In fact, the most senior leaders and client leaders across a great many service companies can do little to help ensure the retention of your best team members.

To show why, let's break down the three problem statements above and turn them on their head.

- **People quit if they think their direct boss is a dolt.**

The solution to this is simple. If you are a leader in your organization, you simply can't allow people who manage teams to be anything less than a top performer. With leaders, you can't simply measure their contributions; you must measure their leadership competency.

- **People quit if they don't understand the mission and vision of the company and, further, if they don't understand what role their contributions play in that vision.**

Your job as a leader is to translate and hand down what you hear at leadership meetings from the CEO or your most senior leader. When you get to attend that leadership off-site or receive the goals for the year, don't just consume those documents—share and distribute them, and make sure your team members understand what they say.

- **People quit if they can't get their best work done because of artificial barriers like politics, too many meetings, or silly permissions.**

Dare to get out the gunk! Is your team filling out reports you don't read? Is your team attending meetings your ex-boss, who quit three years ago, put on the calendar? Do you make your employees justify every dollar they need or want to spend? Be a gunk buster. Make this fun. Send around a "gunk survey."

GUNK SURVEY

- What is the largest frustration in your job?
- On a scale of 1–10 (10 being the highest), how frustrated are you with your ability to get your job done?
- What are the three rituals you do each week that drive you crazy and add no value?
- For your top client/customer, what are the two things you are asked to do that drive zero value?
- If you were not wasting time navigating around roadblocks, what else could you do with this time?
- Explain if you think our organization is political or not.

Be the biggest, most fearless, and unapologetic leader for rotation. In the marketing services industry, we are always tempted to keep our key employees on our key accounts for very reasonable notions that range from consistency to something more guttural, like "Our super important client loves Billy, and we simply cannot take Billy off client X." Well, after many years, Billy begins to realize you care more about client X than him, and he leaves. Now you are not only in trouble with the client, but you lost Billy and his talent went out the door. You both lost. Instead, be brave in rotations. Someone needs to own this process, so until someone else does, it should be you!

Specific Advice on Rotations: Telegraph long in advance to both your client and your employee that you are going to make a change. If it is January and you want to move a key employee in October, then by all means, tell the client and employee in March, a full six months in advance. This will make the transition process easier on the client and will give the employee a very clear tunnel of light ahead.

THREE HABIT CHANGES

1. Vision/Values—make sure you are either creating sensible vision and values if you are on the top leadership team or that you are sharing it out if you're a supervisor. Don't make excuses for why your staff doesn't understand their roles.

2. Rotation Czar—you, even more than HR or the CEO, will know when your lead creative partner, production partner, or media partner needs a rotation. Before you can even ask, the answer is "Yes, yes, you are your brother or sister's keeper." Your ability to advocate for rotations for your partners will ensure that your client has a fresh and excited team, but also that folks see you as someone who is a guardian of culture and people, and not simply a workhorse.

3. Gunk Survey—use the questions here to create your own survey, and don't be afraid to customize it for your own unique team. Do this once every six months. It will help ensure that you never let gunk get in the way of your best employees doing their best work.

YOUR FROM → TO PERSONAL GOAL:

FROM being just another manager at the office, TO being the reason people love coming to work.

ASK QUESTIONS PEOPLE JUST CAN'T PREPARE FOR

"I always take my most important interviews at a bar so I can see how they interact with the crowd, the waitress, and a glass of wine."

—ANTHONY MARTINELLI, CO-FOUNDER OF IGNITIONONE

There are two fundamental reasons why it's so darn hard to interview for Great Client Partners:

- Reason 1: The fundamental problem with interviewing for Great Client Partners is that potential candidates over practice and over research for every normal question.
- Reason 2: The actual greatest skills needed to be great in account management—perseverance, grace under

fire, and creativity—are simply not easily interviewed for during a thirty-to-forty-five-minute interview slot.

So what do you do? Well, for starters, stop asking them what their greatest weakness is. Their answers will be full of drivel, but it will be your fault. So ask them three specific questions to find out something real.

How did you make money before the age of twenty-one?

What to look for in an ideal answer: here, we are simply looking for some indication of hustle. If you were on the hustle when you were nineteen, you will hustle when you are thirty-one. Between the ages of twelve and thirty-nine, I sold fireworks in my high school, ran a snow-shoveling business, sold baseball cards, was a runner on the commodities exchange, and was a low-wage worker at a gym. I grew up in an affluent area, meaning I did not hustle for dinner. I hustled because I loved to hustle.

What was a time when you let down a loved one, and what did you learn from it?

What to look for in an ideal answer: can they go off script, be honest, and emote? The question is made to trigger a hesitation, reflection, and then honesty—raw honesty.

What is your life's biggest regret?

What to look for in an ideal answer: can someone tell you something thoughtful that they have learned from, or are they robots who tell you their biggest problem is being a pleaser?

What would you do if you were CEO of your current company?

Look for someone here who is not just a complainer, but someone who has leading thoughts around solutions and someone who has vastness of thinking.

Are you a builder, an evolver, or a caretaker?

Here you are looking to understand: (1) how self-aware that person is; and (2) what their prime mode of operations is.

Sell me this pen.

What to look for in an ideal answer: Is someone a creative thinker? Many people will come up with simple uses that are visually obvious for an object of this size and type, like it's a great solution if you need something to write with. Or, they might get creative and suggest it can be used as a vase. A really creative person melts down the plastic and makes jewelry or rethinks dimension, making the cap a sled for a mouse!

Go up to the whiteboard with a marker and tell me how many Mach 3 razors can be sold each year in the US by doing a market sizing exercise.

What to look for here are a few things: (1) Will this person crumble when given a marker, or will they have a structure to get the answer? (2) Do they know and realize to first ask questions? (3) Do they have a thesis (even if incorrect) to pull through the entire answer?

You aren't limited to these example questions. The point is to ask things that unsettle the candidate. Other subjects would include, "When did you last lose your cool?" or "What do you think is wasteful in the world?" or "Why do you want to work at all?" All of these things get to the root of the candidate's thinking and are prone to show their philosophy.

THREE HABIT CHANGES

1. Ask better questions when interviewing. Use the above list or something that creates a bit of real-life pressure. And know ahead of time what you want to hear from every question you ask.
2. Use your interview time wisely. There's a lot you cannot address because of the time constraints, but if you're prepared, you can at least have a general discussion with the candidate about this limitation, and that discussion can show a lot about their personality.

3. Don't be afraid to get unorthodox when interviewing, and not just with your questions or expected answers, but with your overall approach. Always start by asking how you can change the environment. Don't be afraid to switch things up.

YOUR FROM → TO PERSONAL GOAL:

FROM a leader who asks about strengths and weaknesses, TO a leader who probes deeper to get the best talent.

LESSON 29

ALIGNMENT, ALIGNMENT, ALIGNMENT

If the central thesis of this book, and the crux of working with people in general, is the importance of building trust, then the fundamental question is how do you do that? A book that deals profoundly with this question is David H. Maister's *The Trusted Advisor* (which I referenced back in Lesson 11). It distills the ingredients of trust into three parts:

- Credibility
- Reliability
- Intimacy

The Trusted Advisor is one of the most influential books I have ever read, and I still follow the coauthor's every word and tweet.

However, this equation of credibility, reliability, and intimacy misses out on what I now believe is a very fundamental piece of the equation: alignment.

Without alignment, all is doomed to fail in a client-agency relationship. You can have the pope of account management who is skilled in intimacy creation, deft at being reliable, and more credible than Walter Cronkite, but if there is no alignment, then you are doomed.

So what is alignment and how do you remember that in your client relationships?

Alignment is simply the art of ensuring that the interests, backgrounds, and intentions of both parties are being considered when calculating a move of any type.

Here is what happens when there is poor alignment between an employee and a manager. When I was a younger man, I was the account director for a big pharma account. I had done very well and had grown the account. So, after some time, I approached our president and asked to become the first ever pharma category lead at our agency. For me, it would mean more prestige, a better title, and more responsibility than my peers. I felt very proud of my ask.

But for my president, what would it mean? Well, it turns

out the answer was headaches. Jim looked at me and said, "Jared, this does not align with our strategy or our title structure, and we do not need a vertical lead of pharma."

He was polite but pointed, and I left the room with a bruised ego. But it was my fault. I did not think of mutual alignment. What was in it for my boss or the company? Not enough. There was no alignment.

Financially, it would have benefited me, but it also would have been extra resources the company would have to spend without getting much in return. Hence, no financial alignment.

Emotionally, this would have boosted my self-worth, but it would have confused other employees. It would have caused more headaches. Hence, no emotional alignment.

In terms of focus, this would have focused me on healthcare, but that was not the strategy the company wanted to pursue. Hence, no focus alignment.

Alignment failure.

How to achieve alignment, the core of trust, can be visualized by a triangle with equal weights at all three corners. Those three corners of alignment are: financial, emotional, and focus.

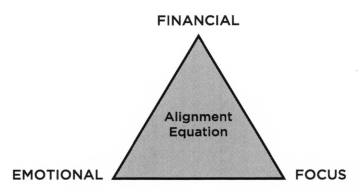

FINANCIAL

Alignment
Equation

EMOTIONAL

FOCUS

Financial: There are two parties in every financial equation: the buyer and the seller. You can pretend to be partners all you want, but this is almost never the case in the services industry without meaningful investment. However, whichever side of this dynamic you are on, understand that your only goal is to create mutual alignment in the financial arrangement. For a services business, financial alignment is relatively simple. The client needs to receive a service at a rate they are comfortable paying, and the agency must be able to profit. Actually, the agency profiting is in the best interests of the client because a healthy agency provides better work for the client.

Emotional: If you are reading this and you're in the creative services industry, then you understand you are in the enthusiasm business. Emotional alignment simply means that both parties care roughly in equal measures about the assignment. If a client has a launch of a new bacon product, the team better feel as though this is the single coolest and most innovative food launch ever.

Focus: Focus alignment simply is the notion that the agency and the client are both zeroed in on the task at hand. The work has to be equally important to both client and agency, and the mutual investment must also be one that ensures importance. To aid in focus alignment, I would caution that the staffing model must indicate that a vast number of folks in the staffing model are at least 75 percent. Only if that is the case will the client feel equal parts focus. This is because in the agency business, too often staffing models are built in such a way where focus is not a possibility. I can tell you from experience that when Billy, the media planner, is 8 percent staffed on a client's business, that simply does not allow for focus. For a typical midsized media engagement, we tend to see the left column (from the following chart) play out. Instead, I would argue that FTE allocations need to be far greater, as indicated in the right column.

	TYPICAL STAFFING MODEL	FOCUS ALIGNMENT
Account Director	15%	50%
Group Media Director	30%	50%
Media Supervisor	50%	100%
Media Manager	25%	100%
Media Coordinator	25%	100%
Data Analyst	10%	50%
Project Manager	5%	25%

How does this create focus alignment? Simple. Every morning, the team represented in the right column is only, or mostly, waking up with that client's business on their mind, and not projects for eight other clients.

Focus, focus, focus.

Alignment, alignment, alignment.

THREE HABIT CHANGES

1. Before proposing any changes, consider if your motives are aligned with the motives of everyone else the change will affect. It helps to take out a pen and make a list of what you want and why.
2. When evaluating a key client relationship, take out the Alignment Triangle and do a brief audit to see how well you are aligned financially, emotionally, and from a focus perspective.
3. Find a way to use the Alignment Triangle, directly or indirectly, to build trust with your clients. After you audit the relationship, let the client know you understand their goals and that you share them.

YOUR FROM → TO PERSONAL GOAL:

FROM being a leader who looks for wins from only your perspective, TO always thinking about mutual alignment.

LESSON 30

UNDERSTAND THE PROFOUND DIFFERENCE BETWEEN THE FYI AND BANGING THE DESK

Client Partners need to be self-aware. What they don't see very often is how they are judged by executive management, but their ability to understand those impressions will define their careers.

One of the biggest beefs execs have with client partners is the manner by which bad news moves up the chain. The expectation gap is that a client partner thinks they have put management on high-alert about a problem, while management believes it is just a small issue. As an aspiring client leader, you have three modes available to you, but it's essential to understand the differences about what each one is, what they signal, when to use them, and how to follow up.

THE FYI

What it is: The FYI lets someone know about a situation. It's often misused as a CYA (cover your ass), but it can be proactively effective if used early enough.

How to use it: The right way to use it is in advance of an activity or immediately after something happens, which that person would benefit from knowing. It's passive. It's helpful. It's even important.

What it signals: The FYI does not create urgency. It simply lets the recipient know that something is going on. Your FYI, even if a shout for help in your head, is not taken as such by a busy leader.

RAISING THE RED FLAG

What it is: This is a tool to foreshadow that there is a problem. Perhaps your client is ninety days late on payment and you want to tell your CFO. Perhaps you have a client that is dropping signals they are looking for another solution, and you want to raise it urgently to your CEO. This is when you raise the red flag.

How to use it: A red flag should come with an urgent-sounding email that speaks about risks, a risk mitigation plan, what dollar value is at risk, and what help you need from management.

How to follow up: Put a time box in the original communication. Indicate that you are giving the situation thirty days and no more to come to a conclusion, and then you will revisit the problem. Without a time box, there is no signal of urgency or end in sight.

What it signals: There is a problem. It needs work to solve, and soon.

BANGING THE DESK

What it is: This is what you do when there is a major issue, a fork in the road. This is what you do when the creative you are presenting in a few hours is horrible and one more slip up will lose the client's confidence. You go to your chief creative officer and you bang the freaking desk.

How to use it: sparingly.

How to follow up: It's immediate. Rapid and constant follow-up. Texts, in-person visits, and hounding of those who need to be hounded. Don't wait for someone to get back to you, hound everyone until you can't hound anyone else.

What it signals: There is a fire, a major issue, and clients and revenue are in danger.

In my career, I have seen far too many people think they are banging the desk when, in fact, they are raising a red flag. We had a very important client in the financial services industry for a long time. We were in the midst of creating a brand new website for them, and we were two months past deadline. Our leader on the account wrote me a pleasant email in which he told me he officially needed to "raise the red flag," because the site was so late and because costs had now overrun those afforded in the SOW.

However, this was not a red-flag situation. This should have been a desk bang, and it should have occurred two months earlier. Three months earlier, perhaps, he could have raised a red flag, asking for more resources or input on the deadline priorities. A month before that, an FYI would have been appropriate.

THREE HABIT CHANGES

1. Discuss escalation procedures with your direct reports. Do they understand the differences between the FYI, the red flag, and banging the desk?

2. Hold a fire drill. Invent a situation in which you need to go bang the desk, and actually go through the motions with your team. Not only will this teach your team about the expectations for behavior in the case of an emergency, but it will also inure them to the potentially uncomfortable behaviors inherent in those situations.

3. As a manager, create an environment where it's acceptable (and applauded) for your direct reports to bang the desk without fear.

YOUR FROM → TO PERSONAL GOAL:

FROM covering your ass, TO banging the desk

LESSON 31

THE HARD THINGS ABOUT HARD THINGS FOR LEADERS

I have been inspired by an incredible book called *The Hard Thing About Hard Things* written by Ben Horowitz. It's a great book for any aspiring Great Client Partner. It discusses the trials and tribulations of entrepreneurism. Unlike so many famous leadership books where things are always sunny and seventy-two degrees, this particular book shows the underbelly of business really accurately. It got me thinking about the hard things related to client leadership and how they need to be discussed bluntly.

There are specific things that you have been trained to do as an account person. These include:

- Things that are routine (i.e., status sheets)

- Things that have a recipe (i.e., how to present)
- Things that have frameworks (i.e., the four Cs)
- Things that are easy to coach/correct (i.e., professionalism)

And then there are some things that are harder to learn. Here are the hard things about those hard things.

HAVE A FOIL

Our moms, brothers, and best friends all tell us what we want to hear. Your grandma always tells you how good-looking you are. As account folks, we relish that positive feedback. (Hey, it's the truth.) Our review scores and test scores cement what we want to believe—that we are all perfect snowflakes and brilliant in every way. Account people by nature crave positive reinforcement. We need to know we are snowflakes and wonderful and unique in every way.

Actually, what you don't need is another person telling you how great you are. What you do need is a foil, a truth teller. I am lucky enough to have several foils. One is Scott Daly. Scott is smart, he is a contrarian, and he is never afraid to provide advice. This advice is a gift, even if I don't always want to hear it. For a long time, I was of the personal belief that hiring folks directly out of college was a potential financial risk. Scott played my foil and helped me to understand that he and his team can train them up and also recruit college graduates faster. He was not content to just listen; he wanted to be part of a better and different tomorrow. He cared only about the solution. He is a great foil.

If you are going to eat crow, don't nibble.

As discussed briefly in Lesson 24 about communicating without obfuscating, we are conditioned to ease our clients and internal partners into bad news. We phase things. We drivel out details. We drop breadcrumbs. We love to say things like, "It's just another small iteration that's left." We hope things will get better when we know they will get worse. It's the human account-leader condition. This is wrong. When you have bad news or something tough to do, take care of it once with decisiveness, compassion, and honesty. Then move on to the next play.

If people understand the cause, they will work harder for it.

Client leaders are trained to explain, measure, and judge the task at hand. This is unfortunate because the task alone is not motivating. Account managers (especially younger ones) forget to share the cause with the team. The cause (i.e., what it is you are fighting for) is the reason someone should care enough to find another gear in their drive to succeed. Too often, managers assume an employee should not hear the cause for some reason or another. This is almost always a mistake. Taking an extra minute to explain why something is important will mean an extra hour's worth of energy from those working the problem. Do you have a minute to spare in order to gain an hour back? Always try to share the cause with your troops.

There is war time and peace time. Don't confuse the two.

Remember the Accurate Fire Prediction Ratio? Client leaders have to understand when they are at war and when they are at peace. Not knowing which one you are in the midst of means certain death for your team. When you get that FedEx note that you lost the business, it was because you failed to see you were at war in the first place. War means entirely different behaviors, work levels, team needs, investment, and executive-level escalation. War means you need a battle plan that ends in victory. Understand when you are at war and act accordingly.

Being a good person still matters.

Client leaders need to be a positive influence. Positivity and genuine interest can't be sometimes things; they must be all-the-time things. If you are in a meeting, be all the way in the meeting.

At the age of twenty-seven, I was a high-flying account director at Avenue A. I was the youngest AD in the company, and in my head, I was hot stuff. I definitely allowed a bit of success to get to my head, and it affected my behaviors.

Torrence Boone, our GM, had an associate from his days at Bain Consulting come in to share a bit about a new technology related to rich media. I reluctantly joined the meeting as a favor, and from minute one, I was terrible. I was a skeptic. I ambushed the meeting with tactical, nitpicky questions about the technology and managed to find everything that could be wrong. And that was only the first half of the meeting. During the second half of the meeting, I was distracted and zoned out, and then, to make matters worse, I left early.

Somehow this got back to Torrence. He hauled me back into his office and simply told me to stop acting like a punk. He went on to remind me that my personal brand was always being evaluated and that I was an ambassador not just for the agency, but for our clients at every turn. I am so thankful he told me I was becoming a punk.

My hope is that you ask yourself these six questions so you, too, can work to ensure you're not being a punk. It's like my Grandpa Burt told me, "Always show respect to the cashiers of the world and be a man of character." Put forth your best self.

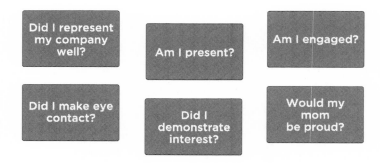

THREE HABIT CHANGES

1. Treat vendors like you wish to be treated. If Facebook or Google is in your office, you show up on time, turn off your iPhone and focus. Do this for non-behemoth businesses, too.

2. Find someone who will debate with you at least once a month. Literally, having a foil is so key that if you don't have this naturally, seek it out.

3. When asking your teams to do something over and above, always try and explain the cause. Be clear about what is at stake and what the benefit is to the agency and team.

YOUR FROM → TO PERSONAL GOAL:

FROM being comfortable only during the good times, TO embracing chaos and making it your ladder.

CONCLUSION

Recently, I was having lunch with a colleague in the advertising industry who told me a story about a rock and a watermelon who get in a fight. He said that whether the watermelon hits the rock or the rock hits the watermelon, the watermelon is going to be on the losing end.

And so it goes for folks in the agency, marketing services, and consulting business, right? It's said that the clients have all the power and the agency folks take the orders.

Clients want partners, not simply service. I believe clients don't want to just be the rock, making all the decisions, ordering you around, pulverizing you into a smashed watermelon. I believe clients want their accounts managed, not just whims catered to. I believe that great agency folks are an extension of great client teams. I believe a

Great Client Partner can revolutionize their own agency and the clients with whom they are privileged to work.

As CEO of 360i, one of the top integrated communication agencies in the US, I get to see a lot of RFPs (Requests for Proposals). When you sift out words like "the," the most common word in these documents tends to be "partner." Clients, as RFPs go, are looking for a partner. At least, the best of the best clients know they are more likely to win by surrounding themselves with strong, smart, opinionated partners and advocates.

These raw and essential qualities that make up great leaders are, in fact, very real, and they're most definitely something that can be bought, taught, and learned. A great account person is truly someone who can differentiate an agency/consultancy or company in the eyes of a client. I reject the idea that anyone is born with these skills. They most assuredly are nurtured, taught, and trained. Practice, repeat, and most of all, teach some young twenty-three-year-old named Billy how to do this—and remind him it's not simply innate, but something that can be learned and refined. Everything can be learned. Everything.

THANKS

Jeanine is by far the best thing I have gotten out of working in the marketing world. I met her at Avenue A, married her shortly thereafter, and have never looked back. I love the life we have built together after more than a decade of being married, and I love her more now than when she first sat down in the row of seats right behind me in the summer of 2001. Without her I would not have this job, not only because she was my initial connection to the job itself, but because she has helped me realize at every turn that I could accomplish anything I set out to. She has a way of believing I can do things that even I am unsure of. She has been my biggest supporter and has pushed me at every turn too. A great partner does both. I certainly have missed my share of moments at home due to big pitches and client visits, and so very often she does the hard work in our house when those moments arise. I am thankful for it all. My life is never dull at work, and Jeanine has a certain spark that ensures it's never dull at home.

My son, Avner, and my daughter, Alex, are always an inspiration to me. I marvel at the obstacles they overcome. I watch how they are so curious, so creative, and so kind, and I smile and remember how lucky I am. I am very proud of them, and I know they will achieve incredible things as they continue to grow up. My son, Avner, has unrelenting curiosity, energy, a big heart, and a ton of perseverance. My daughter, Alex, has a smile that lights up any room, creativity that is off the charts (she is also an author), a love of learning, and she can see the good in anybody and any situation.

To my mom, dad, sister, cousins, aunts, uncles, and grandparents, you have all taught me for years the value of trust and how long-lasting and loving relationships take work and compromise but are all that matter. I love you all very much and am lucky to have such an amazing family.

I want to thank some of my most important mentors over the years, many of whom are mentioned in this book: Jim Warner, Jason Trevisan, Torrence Boone, Diahann Young, Stuart Kronauge, and Bryan Wiener. I have also been pushed by my closest friends and peers both in the industry and outside of it: Jon Weinbach, Jeff Helman, Jordan Schecter, Ben Wolf, Eric Edell, Justin Goldman, Rich Hollman, Brian Fox, Dave Kashen, Michael Cohn, Jon Rosenthal, Barry Medintz, Michael Morrissey, Vipul Kapadia, Anthony Martinelli, Will Margiloff, Roger Barnette, Sarah Hofstetter, and my buddies in the Benjamins.

I want to thank Laura Hoistad who helped to make this book a reality. Finally, thank you to everyone at 360i (past and present) who help make this place magical.

ABOUT THE AUTHOR

JARED BELSKY is CEO of 360i, a top advertising agency in the US that has helped its clients capitalize on industry changes. During his ten-year tenure, Jared has led the agency's growth, guiding product development and overall strategic direction, in addition to overseeing 360i's Media practice. Under Jared's leadership, 360i has been named Adweek's Breakthrough Media Agency of the year, repeatedly ranked among the best Lead Agencies and Search Agencies by Forrester Research, and featured in Ad Age's coveted A-List issue for eight consecutive years.

As CEO, Jared leverages his integrated vision to define what the modern agency model looks like and to drive innovation at scale on behalf of 360i's client partners. Jared has spearheaded 360i's industry-leading expertise in Voice, including the development of Voice Search Monitor (VSM) software that reverse-engineers algorithms used by the most prevalent Voice platforms to help brands stay top-of-mind in all forms of discovery. Before he was CEO, Jared served as the agency's president for five years and cultivated a client-first organization, overseeing 360i's global Search, Analytics, and Media (Display, Programmatic and Paid Social) practice.

Jared was named to Advertising Age's "40 Under 40" in 2017, honored as "Executive of the Year" at the 2016 Bing Awards, on Adweek's Media All-Star list in 2014, and has served as a trusted advisor to world-class brands like Capital One, H&R Block, Norwegian Cruise Lines, and others.

Prior to joining 360i, Jared had over a decade of marketing experience, which includes the launch of a new CPG brand, managing marketing for Coca-Cola's Fanta brand, and working in media buying and account roles as one of the first employees at Avenue A (now SapientRazorfish).

Jared received an MBA from Emory University in Marketing and Management and a BA with Honors from the University of Pennsylvania.